TRIBUTE

To

Andy Whitfield
1971-2011

From
His Friends & Fans

Materials collected for this tribute come from the public record
and from submissions directly from the writers. They are offered in
remembrance of Andy Whitfield and those whose lives he touched.

Cover Design: Antelope Design
Cover photo: Vashti Whitfield
Illustrations:
Dawings by Beatriz Suarez Diez
Image of Tattoo Art from Joanna Sharif-Crawley
Collage by Pam Stewart

www.pronghornpress.org

*In remembrance of a man who touched
so many lives through his work and
by simply being himself.*

Foreword

September 11th will always be marred by the tragedies of 2001. Now, with the passing of Andy Whitfield, it is stained in 2011, as well.

This book contains a compilation of messages that pay homage to an extraordinary human being. He has blown us away in his roles as Spartacus and Gabriel. He has shown us humility, strength and grace in the direst of circumstances.

Through his acting, interviews, video clips, photographs and statements by fellow cast members and friends we were inspired by and have come to love Andy.

The following messages are a tribute, written from the heart, by fans all over the globe. May they bring comfort and fond memories to all who love him.

With much love,

—Irena Kyd, M.D.
Reiki Master, New York

All proceeds from the sale of this book will go to the Andy Whitfield Trust Account, HSBC Bank Australia.

Acknowledgments

First and foremost my thanks go to Starz Entertainment LLC for bringing *Spartacus* to the screen and letting Steven DeKnight work his magic with his brilliant writing. Accolades go to each and every one of the cast members for their passionate and authentic portrayal of life in ancient Rome, and to the all hardworking departments for making it seem so beautiful and so real.

My deepest gratitude goes to Louise Rahr and Penny Douglas for creating a forum where we all can share our opinions, our feelings, memories and even lives! Penny is the core of the wonderful Andy Whitfield (AKA "Spartacus") Official Fan Page on Facebook and I can't thank her enough for her support.

Thanks go to Beatriz Suarez Diez for her incredible artwork based on *Spartacus, Blood and Sand.*

I am very grateful to Annette Chaudet of Pronghorn Press for her time and generous offer to publish the book at her expense.

And last, but not least, many thanks to all the special people who shared their thoughts and publicly posted such profound tributes.

May they be an inspiration to Andy's family, friends and fans.

—Irena Kyd
New York

TRIBUTE

To

Andy Whitfield
1971-2011

From
His Friends & Fans

Andy Whitfield 1971-2011

TRIBUTE

A Word from STARZ

A Champion on Screen,
A Legend in our Hearts.

We are deeply saddened by the loss of our dear friend and colleague, Andy Whitfield.

We were fortunate to have worked with Andy in *Spartacus* and came to know that the man who played a champion on-screen was also a champion in his own life. Andy was an inspiration to all of us as he faced this very personal battle with courage, strength and grace.

Our thoughts and prayers are with his family during this difficult time. He will live on in the hearts of his family, friends and fans.

—*Chris Albrecht*
STARZ CEO and President
Press Release

Andy Whitfield 1971-2011

TRIBUTE

From the Spartacus Family

No words to express the depth of such a loss.
You will be deeply missed, my brother.

—*Steven S. DeKnight*
Creator of *Spartacus*

RIP Andy Whitfield, our true champion! You will be incredibly missed! I feel very honored to have known such a person in my life. Today marks a very sad day! Please join in sending him and his family our love & prayers!

—*Nick E Tarabay*
(Ashur)
from his Facebook page

Andy Whitfield 1971-2011

Don't let your fire go out, spark by spark, in the hopeless swamps of the approximate, the not quite, the not yet, the not at all. Do not let the hero in your soul perish, in lonely frustration for the life you deserved, but have never been able to reach. Check your road and the nature of your battle. The world you desired can be won. It exists, it's real, it's possible, it's yours.
—Ayn Rand, *Atlas Shrugged*

Much love to you, Brother, and to your family.
My thoughts and love are with you all.
Endless Respect.

—Dan Feuerriegel
(Agron)

Obviously, Andy Whitfield left an indelible mark on all of us in the *Spartacus* family. He was a gentle man who never said a bad word about anyone, a gifted photographer, engineer (no really!) and a brilliant actor. Andy's incandescent film presence made men want to be him and women want to marry him. Andy's two babies will always know that their Daddy cherished them and their mother, Vashti, above all things. How lucky we were to have him grace all our lives.

Godspeed, Andy!

—Lucy Lawless
statement to EW

TRIBUTE

Andy had a great spirit and was a true warrior. It was great working with such a talented actor, who was a kind family man with a down to earth nature. It was a pleasure witnessing his performance as Spartacus, and was a regular reminder to continue working hard in a career that I love.

Andy will be missed, but has left a legacy behind that will not be forgotten.

—*Kyle Pryor*
(Marcus)

We lost a beautiful soul; words cannot express my sadness. It is a difficult time for Andy's family and out of respect for them, I hope you understand if I do not comment any further. Thank you.

—*Lesley-Ann Brandt*
from her Facebook page

Rest peacefully Andy. You will be sorely missed. Long may you live in our hearts.

—*Gareth Williams*
(*Gods of the Arena*, Vettius)
found on ausxip

Andy Whitfield 1971-2011

I am very saddened at the passing of the beautifully talented Andy Whitfield. My thoughts are with his family.

—*Jessica Grace Smith*
(Diona) from her Facebook page

Farewell to a most heroic man and dear friend. Rest in peace, Andy.

—*Viva Bianca*
from her Facebook page

Love.

—*Katrina Law*
(from her Facebook page)

So sad Andy Whitfield lost his fight.
Beautiful, inspiring man.

—*Jamie Murray*
(Gaia)
found on ausxip

TRIBUTE

Will remember you always.

—*Ande Cunningham*
(Duro)
found on ausxip

Goodbye, Andy Whitfield. You were an awesome actor. You will be missed. You even made me want to kill Gauls for a fat, foul Roman emperor.

—*Ted Rami*
Producer
found on ausxip

Andy, there are no words. You were heroic in life, you will never be forgotten.

—*Liam McIntyre*
found on ausxip

Thank you for the kind words about Andy. He was one of the most beautiful people I've ever known— so compassionate, so loving to his friends, family and all who were honored to know him. His untimely passing is devastating.

Please take a moment to love one another.

—*Erin Cummings*
from her Facebook page

Andy Whitfield 1971-2011

It's exciting to be back for season two, but aso it's very difficult to have moved on from Andy Whitfield. And I just want to say a big 'Hello,' to Vashti and to Jesse and Indigo. Be very proud of your father. He was a champion and he was our Spartacus and we loved him very much. We were very proud of him and we were very priviledged to have worked with him.

—*Manu Bennett*
Access Hollywood interview
on the red carpet at the
Spartacus, Season 2 big screen premier

TRIBUTE

Tributes from the Fans

Dearest Vashti, Indigo, and Jesse,

It is with all of my heart that I write this letter to you now. You don't know me at all, unless you read about some of the events that I had put together for Andy, just wanting to try to make a difference in some small way. I want you to know that my heart is broken for you, and all of Andy's family and friends. I know he was your Andy, and always will be, but please allow me this kindness, to say "our Andy" because he was to me and so many others, Our Andy, too. I can only imagine how you must be feeling. I know that it is a very private and personal thing for you all, but I and so many others loved him so very much and just want to share with you how much he meant to us all. It is with all of my

Andy Whitfield 1971-2011

heart and love that I write to you, to tell you how I feel. I lost my Mom to cancer several years ago and it was so hard for me, too.

From the very first time that I saw Andy, when *Spartacus* first aired here in the USA, I thought to myself, there is something very special and extraordinary about this man. I told everyone, my son, my sister, everyone who would listen, that there was this amazing guy on *Spartacus*, and that he was the most amazing person. Without saying a word, he conveyed so much powerful and beautiful emotion. His presence just jumped out of the screen and in to my heart and I knew from that very first moment that he was very unique. He showed so much heart, passion, intensity in his face, with his entire being, and he did it without even saying a word. I felt it deep within my soul. People who didn't watch the show thought I was crazy that I actually felt this way over someone I had never met, but I didn't care what they thought!

I knew better.

Andy was a very bright spot in a very dark time in my life, the worst that things had been in many years and it was very comforting to hear his voice and see him. *Spartacus* was my favorite show and then I also saw him in Gabriel, and even in that role, I felt his same special aura. That rare gift he had was something so soothing, his voice, his passion, all illuminating the screen! I know you already know it, because he was the love of your life. I guess the more I watched him, the more I loved him as a great human being, a very kind, amazing person in this world!

I had just begun to get on Facebook, so I didn't know about starting a fan page of any kind. I did find one that was started by another girl and I joined it and we all talked about him and about the show! I was on there all the time, and now am an admin for the page. I found many who felt the same as me and I have spoken to people all over the world as a result.

There is even a group of ladies, ten of us, who have become best friends because of our love for Andy. We are planning a trip to Australia and New Zealand next year. It was right after Season one had finished airing here in the USA, that we were told that Andy had cancer and that he was going through treatments and would not return. I was just so sad to hear it, like everyone else who loved him. I just couldn't believe it was happening. I prayed and hoped and then a breakthrough came. It was said he was completely healed and well. Then Starz announced that Andy would be at the Comic Con in San Diego in 2010, I was so excited that we would get to hear from him. Starz also had announced that they were having a Fan Chat and there were thousands of questions submitted for him and a few of the cast mates, and only about twelve or fourteen questions actually got asked that day, in a one hour chat. I was so lucky enough to get my question picked and to top it off it was one to Andy!

I will cherish that for the rest of my life. He was just so peaceful, so glad to be there and I was so hopeful. He was going to be back! We were all so excited again! We had hope restored! He was planning to be in Season 2 of *Spartacus*. He was fired up, he said, as were we all. Everything was on a high note again. All of the cast was there; Lucy, John, Viva, Jai, and of course Steven DeKnight was with them, hosting the chat. We all were very pleased to see how good Andy looked and they all were having a lot of fun.

Then more bad news came again. It was within a few months only that we were all told that the cancer had returned and he was going to have to seek more aggressive treatments. I was once again very sad and I can only imagine how you all felt. I want you to know that all of us were so hopeful that he would get well. If he never came back to *Spartacus*, I just wanted to see him well. I put together a "Prayer Event for Andy Whitfield" page on Facebook, and fans all over the world who wanted to could join us for prayer and leave their well wishes and feelings.

I ran those for months on end, and I believed so much in his his complete recovery. During all of those months, his cast mates were all on Facebook and I had been talking to them when I could, and I know that Viva, Nick, Katrina, Manu, and Lesley-Ann all said they gave him the news of the messages and the support and love! It was a glimmer of hope that he could get those messages, that it would give him hope, comfort and uplift him and his family.

It was actually in 2010 when he was first diagnosed that Lesley-Ann had agreed to take our messages to him and we all sent them to her and she printed them and took them to Andy.

That little bit of hope got us through, and then when he came to Comic Con, he mentioned that the messages had really helped him, to lift him up! I really hope that I made just a tiny bit of a difference for him.

I know that you are the love of his life and you are a very strong lady, Vashti, and you and the children were his life! I thank you for sharing him with us, for even that small time. I will be forever grateful to you for it.

I will never forget getting the news from a buddy of mine who is in the show and who had his Mom message me on Facebook. I was told not to tell anyone, so I didn't, until the news started to break all over the net. I was literally in shock and so heartbroken. I was online talking to others and people were freaking out.

To tell you of the love and the overwhelmingly amazing something-out-of-this-world, and the only explanation is that although none of us wanted to lose him, I guess God must have needed him more.

I think Andy is an Angel and I know that on the other side, he is in peace. He didn't want to go, I know that. I want to tell you that he will not ever be forgotten, always will be

TRIBUTE

missed, loved by all, an inspiration to millions, and the world seems much less bright with his passing. I wish and hope that my letter will help you to know, that although we cannot be there to hug you, there are so many who want to do something for you, starting with huge hugs and sending you and the children, Indigo and Jesse, lots of love, continued prayers and well wishes to comfort you through the days, months, years, and the rest of this life.

His cast and all who worked with him on *Spartacus* loved him so much, and I am amazed by their love and care for Andy. It is because of them that I feel that we even had a chance to be able to let him know how we felt, because otherwise, it would have been unlikely. It meant so much to me, personally, and I will always have a place in my heart for Andy. He is a legend. I just cried and cried and still do at his passing, and I will always love him as if he were the brother I never had, the friend I could have only imagined, and an Angel I shall look forward to seeing when I get to the other side.

I don't mean to go so long and I could write a book about all of this, but I will, for sure, write about Andy in my life story. I will send you a copy when I get it done.

Vashti, Andy loved you all so much and I love you, too. Indigo and Jesse, when you get older and you read this, I want to tell you how much your Dad loved you both. He was an amazing human being and he was loved by all of us. Love never dies and so our love will always be there. Your Dad is watching over you, and his love for you will never die, it will last throughout eternity, through the ages!

I want to tell you all that if I never ever get to see you, I will carry such a very special place in my heart for you all.

Andy would want his family to be happy and looked after and I know you have many who love you all and are there with you and around you who will do that. I wish that I could be there and hug you all, and since I cannot, I wanted to write you to tell you how much Andy meant to me and what I felt about all that he gave to us.

I hope that this can help you and that this Tribute book will comfort you very much.

Thank you for listening to my part of this and I want you all to know that I love you, that I care, and that I will not ever forget!

May God be with you all, give you peace, and the comfort that you all are loved by all of us.

With my heart to yours and with all of my love,

—Penny Douglas
Many, Louisiana, USA

What can I say... that he was perfect, that he made everyone else around him a better person by just knowing him or that he made great men seem smaller in his presence. That his silly grin made you smile by just looking at him; all I know for sure is that it is a lesser planet now that he is gone...

I will miss him.

—Danny Miller
a friend and great admirer from Canada

TRIBUTE

Andy Whitfield? An angel, a beloved husband and a great father, you are a great man...you are the best! I wanted you in this world, full of life and health...but I wonder how these last days for you and your beautiful family were. I was so far from you, but you know, I felt so close to you always. I would have liked to take your hand and tell you I love you.

I know the distance between your world now and ours does not help, your physical condition and ours is different...but we'll take care of your children, Jesse Red and Indigo Sky, we'll all remember their father...because their father is special, and because you gave them life...And Vashti, an amazing woman, your beloved wife...I pray for her, it is not easy to rebuild a life without the one you love!

Andy, we love you!

—*Lidia E. García*
Gran Canaria, Spain

A most beautiful man has left our lives...our hearts are broken in two. Andy, there is a space in my life where you once stood never to be filled...you were so respected by everyone...a beautiful and talented young man. I, for one, will miss you soooo much.

I can't imagine the pain and grief your family is going through. Vashti has lost her soulmate and Jesse and Indigo have lost their beloved father, but I know that Vashti will keep your memory alive in those two darling little children and tell them every day what a wonderful talented human being their daddy was and how much he was loved by thousands of people all over the world. This book will prove it.

Your passing feels very personal to me. I only found you for a short while, but I feel like I've known you all my life. You touched my heart with your terrific acting and your zest for life which was taken from you.

I still pray for you Andy, that you are now at peace. I pray for Vashti, Jesse and Indigo. I pray to God to give her strength to carry on and I send her love every day. I still cry for you Andy, my life will never be the same. The world is a sadder place without you in it. Love and respect will always be yours. I'm sending a big bear hug from me to you because I love you; you will always be my champion and my hero.

I am really sad right now so I will go. Much love to you, Andy, forever in my heart.xxxxxx

—Irene Mahon
London, England

Andy leaves his screen presence, his energy, his beauty and his strength, his "everything," as a precious and eternal legacy to all of us!

—Rosario
Italy

TRIBUTE

We wanted more and more of you, of your acting skills, of your full and passionate dedication to achieve your dreams, of your stunning and sexy presence, of your charming and magic touch, of your wonderful soul and hypnotic dreaming eyes that made us live all kinds of emotions...more of what you really have been gifting us during this time. Now it's so hard to come to the sad reality of such a tragic and undeserved fate, but you will always be remembered as the perfect special man we all dream about, the greatest of the fighters, a loving father and husband and the best of actors in a long time. No one like you Mr. Whitfield, neither before nor after. I will always keep hanging onto your charm and I will keep on watching your beautiful pictures and superb performances, which I keep as a treasure, each time I want to feel in heaven.

Love you, Mr. Whitfield, and will miss you for the rest of my life, forever in my heart, my brave warrior. I hope your light finds my soul in the afterlife.

—Inés
Seville, Spain

Spartacus will not be the same without you. The character captured my heart and thoughts. Very talented indeed. Thoughts are with your family and friends.

—Anna
Cheshire, England

Andy Whitfield 1971-2011

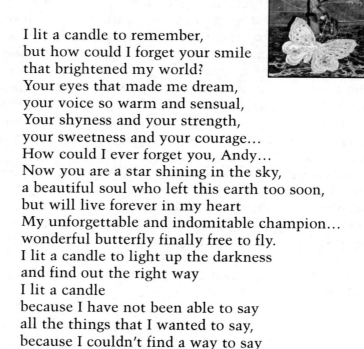

I lit a candle to remember,
but how could I forget your smile
that brightened my world?
Your eyes that made me dream,
your voice so warm and sensual,
Your shyness and your strength,
your sweetness and your courage...
How could I ever forget you, Andy...
Now you are a star shining in the sky,
a beautiful soul who left this earth too soon,
but will live forever in my heart
My unforgettable and indomitable champion...
wonderful butterfly finally free to fly.
I lit a candle to light up the darkness
and find out the right way
I lit a candle
because I have not been able to say
all the things that I wanted to say,
because I couldn't find a way to say
how much I love you...

Goodbye Andy...May God bless you and your
family! May you find peace and serenity in heaven,
completely free of suffering, surrounded by the love of
us all...

I miss you, Andy...I'm Gonna Miss You Forever...

—*Paola Olioso*
Pescara, Italy

TRIBUTE

We did not LOSE him, he was TAKEN from us!

He was the sun, never to shine again. Yet, we are the fortunate ones. How infinitely larger is the grief, oh, the grief! for his family. An anniversary with no husband. Birthdays with no daddy. Holidays with no son or brother.

We are fortunate to have seen a few precious hours of that glorious man, to have tasted his passion and have heard his voice. That voice...it can only be called divine.

I am trying hard to be grateful, to be reasonable...

I am not succeeding.

I still ask why? WHY?

—Fulvia Severina
New York, USA

Dearest Vashti,

When this book reaches your hands and you can read it I want you to know that your beloved young husband came into our lives to steal our hearts. Andy is loved all over the world; he is a very special human being. On the day of his departure to paradise, tears filled the seas and rivers of the world!

I offer my respect and my love for staying with him and loving him so deeply to the very end, and please, a kiss from me to those precious jewels, your children, who are a part of Andy in this world. Feel fortunate always, for being the woman who conquered the heart of this man; it belongs to you entirely! Now, with my words I can only say thank you, thank you for having shared Andy with us all. Each of us carries a piece of Andy in our hearts, and he will never be forgotten.

God bless you, Vashti, you and the children. Sending you a hug and much love.

Everything has a beginning and an end, but Andy, even though you're gone forever, you live in me every day. You live in the hearts and minds of all the people in the world who love you.

I miss you so much, sweet Angel of Light!

—Lidia E. García
Gran Canaria, Spain

No one can reach the top armed only with talent.
God gives talent, work transforms talent into genius.
—Anna Pavlova

Andy got to the top and will always be remembered as the actor and great person that captivated us all.

—Begoña García Diez
Zaragoza, Spain

TRIBUTE

Andy was our Heart of Gold
Our light shining in the darkness
And we were drawn to his flame.
But now his flame has been put out
And we wander without purpose.
Lost in shadows, in a world bereft of color.
So we cling to each other in our grief
Finding comfort in each other's broken hearts
Hoping that one day we may see his light again
And tell him face to face in that place of perfect love.
Beloved.

—*Loretta LaRusso*
New York, USA

Andy Whitfield 1971-2011

*If tears could build a stairway
and memories a lane,
I'd walk right up to heaven
and bring you home again.
No farewell words were spoken,
no time to say goodbye.
You were gone before I knew it,
and only God knows why.
My heart still aches with sadness,
and secret tears still flow.
What it meant to love you
no one will ever know.
But now I know you want me
to mourn for you no more,
but remember all the happy times
life still has much in store.
And since you'll never be forgotten,
I pledge to you today
a hollowed place within my heart
is where you'll always stay.*
　　　　　　　—Author Unknown

　　　　　　　　　　　　—D.D. Lichteneiche
　　　　　　　　　　　　Germany

Forgive me, Andy, for all my tears
But my heart aches with so much pain,
Why you, my precious brother?
But no one can explain.
It's life I'm told, it's life
But that doesn't help the pain,
For if I could have one wish,

TRIBUTE

You know I'd make you better again.
You're the one who always knew what to do
You're the one who always kept us together,
You're the one I thought would always be here
To love us forever and ever.
One in a million, that's what you are
Always by our side,
Praying for a miracle each day
So we can all get off this rollercoaster ride.
But my words are not meant to make you sad
I simply just want to say, thank you,
For I'm proud to be your brother
You'll be missed my brother, WE LOVE YOU.

This is for you, my brother. I hope you like it, and know how much you mattered to all of us.

—Glenn Kinley
Rochester, New York

Andy came into my life by chance and will stay in my heart for all eternity. His work, full of emotions and feelings expressed, created in me a precious link, which will last forever.

I was so far from him, but you know, I felt so close, always. Andy accompanies me every day on my walks. Andy accompanies me every day while I'm breathing. Andy is present in my life, because he's the rising sun every day, to enlighten the life in this world! Without having known him personally, he was, he is and will be, part of my heart, forever.

My office of work is next to the sea, and every day I see this immense blue sea, and it reminds me of the wonderful blue eyes of our beloved actor, a man loved around the world, Andy Whitfield, "Spartacus."

The link of love is so great. I wake up every day and he is one of my first thoughts. I would have liked to meet him personally and shake his hand and say how much I loved him!

Andy, we all love you! And Lidia Esther Garcia, your unconditional fan, shouts to you in heaven: "Andy Whitfield, you're here with us, and will never be forgotten!"

—*Lidia E. García*
Gran Canaria, Spain

I first saw Andy Whitfield in Gabriel and I knew immediately he was a rare talent, he had the ability to reach into his audience and make them feel deeply, even with just a glance. I looked forward to watching him become the star I knew he was destined to be. When I learned Andy had lost his battle with cancer, I knew the world is a lesser place because of his passing. I have seen the power of this disease in my own family, but Andy dealt with it with such grace and strength I believed he would beat it. How could such a powerful life force not?

I honor his memory by loving each day and the people in it. I thank Vashti for sharing her husband with us and I hope she knows that we know what a gift that was. I, for one, am grateful. My heart and prayers go out to all the people who knew and loved Andy, especially his wife and beautiful children. We are all better for having known Andy, even though it was for far too short a time.

—*Elizabeth Biggerstaff*
Delmar, New York, USA

TRIBUTE

Andy, you inspire all of us to be better people and to find our dream and live it.

—*Alexis Carril*
Miami, USA

I can't even find the words to describe how the story of a guy from Wales came to be one of the most loved and respected actors who meant the world to his fans and all who knew him. I never knew him except through his work, but when I looked into his eyes I saw a rare and beautiful soul who will always be cherished. To his family I will repeat the words spoken to me in my time of loss: "The love you shared with and for him will get you through anything."
Much love,

—*Carol Cork*
Wolverhampton, West Midlands, UK

Mr. Whitfield,

I just want to say how much I love and miss you, knowing you are not here with us is totally unbearable. But you are now fully healed, no more pain, your beautiful eyes shine once more, the brightest star in our sky. I am so glad to have you in my life, the very thought of you still gives me flutterbys, makes me smile, and you will ALWAYS, ALWAYS be the perfect man to me.
xxxx LOVE YOU ALWAYS xxx

—*Jeannette Smith*
Liverpool, England

Andy Whitfield 1971-2011

A month has passed and still the chains of grief around my heart weigh me down, for you are only in the next room. I wish that you would return in my place, to be with your wife and children. I would still my beating heart to have it replaced by yours. Such pain will always remain, but numbed by time I'm sure. Nothing and no one will ever replace the warrior of our hearts, nor shall we forget the brave battle you fought so gracefully.

We hurt with no relief save for the fact that you're at peace, which brings us a bitter-sweet comfort and to know that you watch over those who love you and who also loved you in return, R.I.P my angel, for we will meet one day. xxx

—Jill 'Dillymoo' Swindell
Newcastle, UK

Andy had something that you cannot teach, learn or become. He was just a remarkable person, who captivated a loyal fan base and truly inspired us all. There has not been a day since his passing that I don't remember him in some way.

You are forever missed. The sky wept with your passing...

—Brian Zeppernick
Dallas, Texas, USA

TRIBUTE

Four weeks have passed since you've gone and all that remains are your pictures and your videos, all that remains is a deep sense of emptiness and sadness, a sense of deep injustice and the regret for what could be and will not be, anymore.

How much I believed that you could do it, how much I believed in a miracle, me, who didn't believe in miracles anymore.

But now you're gone. I know, you're in a better place, now you can rest forever free from pain and suffering, just in peace. But for us who remain, you leave a great void, you leave us here in a world that is a sadder place without you. You leave your photos and the memory of a hero, a beautiful champion who has been taken away too soon.

I Miss You Andy, I Miss You So Much. I'm Gonna Miss You Forever.

—Paola Olioso
Pescara, Italy

Andy, you left us a month ago, but it seems it was today. You're always in my heart. You will be forever remembered as a special man, an extraordinary person and you will be loved all over the world. You will never be forgotten, Andy Whitfield. You are still alive in our minds forever. I miss your smile, your voice on *Spartacus*. You were a Gentleman. You were a MAN and I won't forget you—ever—because you changed my life.

Rest in Peace.

—Lavinia Goretti Carmona
Lisbon, Portugal

Andy Whitfield 1971-2011

In all my thirty-six years I have never been moved or struck by anyone I did not personally know like I was by Andy. To say I am a fan does not seem enough, somehow. A fan might come and go, but we are part of something very special. A lot of people will know what I mean. We watched together, we prayed together, we cried together.

Andy died on my daughter's birthday, so I will forever remember the date. Two weeks later I did something I would never have imagined I would. I got a small intricate tattoo of a butterfly with Andy's initials discreetly woven into its wings. It will be there forever. I hope with all my heart Andy's beautiful wife and children know how very much we think about them and truly care. And to Andy:when I get to Heaven I'll look out for you!

With love...

—*Joanna Sharif-Crawley*
Buckinghamshire, UK

TRIBUTE

To Andy Whitfield's Family and Friends,

May everlasting memories warm your heart and, most importantly, your souls. Carry with you smiles and laughter and when sadness creeps in, close your eyes and hear that laughter.

I wish you Blessings and Happiness in all the days of your lives from which you will then return home to see a loving face waiting for you.

With much love...

—Mikkey T. McCarthy
Drexel Hill, Pennsylvania, USA

More than one month and the certainty of your absence is even more unbearable because the longing we feel for you will never be satiated and so the feeling of discouragement will last forever. Nothing nor nobody will ease this void. Just our endless love and admiration for you, the treasure of your beautiful legacy and the part of you that you left in this world, your children, will help us to endure the sadness of your unreasonable loss. You had so much to give! I will always take you in my heart.

Love and miss you, forever my extraordinary man.

—Inés
Seville, Spain

Andy Whitfield 1971-2011

The Measure of a Man

Not, how did he die, but how did he live?
Not, what did he gain, but what did he give?
These are the units to measure the worth
of a man as a man, regardless of his birth.
Nor what was his church, nor what was his creed?
But had he befriended those really in need?
Was he ever ready, with words of good cheer,
To bring back a smile, to banish a tear?
Not what did the sketch in the newspaper say,
But how many were sorry when he passed away?
                                    —Author Unknown

This poem says everything about Andy! He touched the hearts of everyone through his pure brilliance on screen. His life has been tragically cut short, for reasons beyond our control. Yet he will live on through his beautiful children.
Love to Vashti and family at this incredibly sad time.
xxx

—*Jude*
Plymouth, UK

Andy was an inspiration, and a man of many skills. He will be missed. May his soul rest in peace.

—*Spartacus* Italian Fanpage

TRIBUTE

Your name tattooed on my deep heart...a beautiful butterfly, of blue color. Beautiful memories, in my mind! A beautiful gift, to live your emotions through the screen. Excellent performance in your work made me smile, made me feel, made me mourn, and is the reason you occupy a special place in my life and a place privileged in my heart! Andy to me a special person, an amazing man, a beautiful shade, a color set, the beautiful rainbow! He's a shining star and its nice light, the blue sky, the most beautiful smile, the sun and the light, thousands of hearts, giving love, a universe, a beautiful place to stay and watch your family, your wife and babies. Do not forget: Feel surrounded by the love we send you in heaven, the hope, many prayers!

I pray for you! I pray for your family!! I write for you, I weep for you. You are not here, but you're still here. I do not want to forget, I refuse to forget, because love for you is for ever. I miss you.

My Angel, your light lit me every day!

A fan with much love for you!

—Lidia E. García
Gran Canaria, Spain

A colossal space has been left where you once stood, but be assured it will be guarded with much love. xxx

—Sandra James
Eastcalder, Westlothian, Scotland

Andy Whitfield 1971-2011

I could write something every day since Andy passed, I've thought of him and his family every day. My birthday is September 16 and I couldn't even shake it that one day.

I've loved many people who were ravaged by cancer. My grandmother died of it in 1987 and I'll never forget what she told my mom during the second round of treatment. My mom was caring for her in our home and asked what my grandma wanted, meaning lunch or some tea, and my grandmother answered, "I want to live."

She had raised six children, loved eleven grandchildren and at that time two great grandchildren. She made the best homemade rolls and cookies and Sunday dinners for all of us and it was still too soon to go.

I loved watching Andy perform in *Spartacus*, he brought me so much enjoyment. And from my very far vantage point, watching Andy and getting to learn a little of his spirit, I was crushed when he passed. He was a wonderful person, man, husband, father, and friend. The very little I can offer is that his spirit has encouraged me to continue my daily battle with the diabetes which I've had since I was a child. It is beginning to take a toll on my body and I have a choice, every day, to give in and let the disease take my life or to fight.

Today I fight because I want to live, as I am sure Andy did. Life is not easy, but it is beautiful. Andy reminded me of that when I started to forget.

I pray that God blesses those he left here and I know that we all see our loved ones in the hereafter. He will be waiting for and watching over his loved ones and I am a better person for the little I knew him.

—Elizabeth Biggerstaff
Delmar, New York

TRIBUTE

Vashti,

I want you to know that the big loss that your family has suffered also causes a terrible pain to us all, his fans. I cannot imagine the magnitude of yours in comparison.

After one month I come to the conclusion that not even a million words can ease the pain of the early loss of such a beautiful, exemplary, extraordinary and adorable man, who inspired and moved the hearts of so many people. I know that his memory will always live in my heart as I know, without having met him, that he is a very important person in my life, forever.

I will always admire him as the perfect man and outstanding actor that he was, but more importantly I will always love him and will pray for you and your beautiful children to go through this hard time with the help of the good moments and love that he gave you in life and the knowledge of the huge amount of love that he has promoted all over the world.

—*Inés*
Seville, Spain

Tears are words too painful for a broken heart to speak.
Andy, forever you will live in our hearts.
Love and Miss you so much xx,

—*Jeannette Smith*
Liverpool, England

Hi Vashti,

I was sitting thinking to myself that you must have known months ago that Andy would not make it. My God woman, you must have been going through hell trying to keep everything together—in the beginning both of you, then when Andy became really ill, you had to shoulder everything yourself. What a marvelous and wonderful woman you are!

Andy will always be my hero, but you are now my hero. You are the bravest woman I know, you and Andy's mum, you're both amazing women.

I always dreamed one day I would meet Andy. Now that will never happen. I just wanted to shake his hand, give him

TRIBUTE

a kiss on the cheek and tell him how awesome I thought he was as an actor and a wonderful human being. He touched all our hearts, we all loved him so much. Through Andy I have found the most awesome friends.

With much love and respect to you, Vashti, and your beautiful children...xxxxxxx

—*Irene*
London, England

You proved to be a wonderful actor and it is a real shame you could not enjoy your deserved success. Wherever you are, I want you to know that your interpretation of Spartacus will be retained in our memory forever.

Rest in peace, dear Andy.

—*A. M. Ribeiro*
Madrid, Spain.

I just had a realization I wanted to share: in any photo I see of Andy Whitfield in a group or with anyone else, he always has his arm around someone. That says it all. He always shared himself with love and affection, and maybe this is why we are all so sad about his passing. He hugged us all with his warm spirit.

I hope Vashti and his children still feel his arms around them because I know, whatever is beyond, he keeps them in his embrace.

—*Elizabeth Biggerstaff*
Delmar, New York, USA

Andy Whitfield 1971-2011

Those we love don't go away

They walk beside us everday.

—*Pam Stewart*
Sturbridge, Massachusetts, USA

TRIBUTE

As you release this butterfly in honor of me,
know that I'm with you and will always be.
Hold a hand, say a prayer,
close your eyes and see me there.
Although you may feel a bit torn apart,
please know that I'll be forever in your heart.
Now fly away butterfly as high as you can go,
I'm right there with you more than you know.
—Jill Haley

—*Jeannette Smith*
Liverpool, England

A man fights in the arena, his strength and courage deserve great respect. Spartacus! Andy Whitfield, you're Spartacus for eternity! Your work, the shows, your person, the memory. The best, you are and always will be remembered. But above all, Andy, you are a father and husband respected by all of us.

Thank you for having existed, and for being the brave man we came to know, the true warrior, until the end.

Your eyes are my sky
Your beautiful face is my world
Your great smile is my treasure.

Your family is in my memory too, they're in my prayers and my thoughts daily. Vashti, for you, for your children,much love, strength, hope, the memories, the tears and the joys...live life intensely, every day!

Always, with the best wishes!

—*Lidia E. García*
Gran Canaria, Spain

Andy Whitfield 1971-2011

He died one month ago and I still can't believe it. Such a big loss for everybody. I hope his family will survive this difficult time and get better soon. He will always live in our hearts. What I can do is just wish all the best things to his wife and to the children! We miss you so much Andy!

—*Enik Tóth*
Hungary

Andy was a beautiful humble man who captured millions of hearts all around the world. To Vashti, their two children, Andy's parents and sister: my heart aches for you all. I hope you find comfort in knowing the impact that Andy has left in this world. He will forever remain in our hearts and thoughts.

May your memories bring you all peace.

Love to you all,

—*Teresa Rose*
Tamworth, Australia

An Angel stands by your shoulder, a Butterfly upon your hand, love and adoration surround you to keep you on the right path. Your journey in life was short, but the Legend and your Legacy lives on.

xxx

—*Sandra James*
Eastcalder, Westlothian, Scotland

TRIBUTE

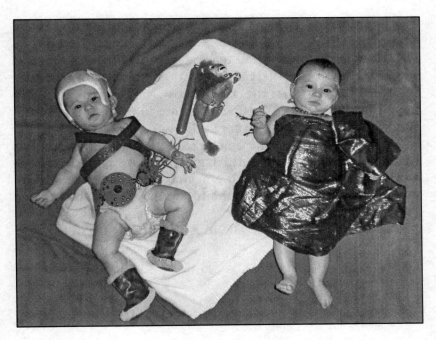

Here I post a photo of my smaller daughters (I have two others, a girl who is six, and a boy who is three). These twins are now ten months old.

Where we live, in Granada, Spain, the weather in June is very hot (around 40°C), so we cannot go outside our home until 9 p.m., so evenings are too long, and we have to think how we can spend time with our children. So, I thought to make this photo.

They are Lucía (dressed up as Spartacus) and Beatriz (Roman girl). Lucía had a plagiocephaly (she is OK now) so she has to wear a helmet. And that's what inspired me to disguise them so…I hope you like it.

Kisses!

—*Elena*
Granada, Spain

Andy Whitfield 1971-2011

I couldn't sleep, so I lit a candle and curled up on the sofa to watch Andy in *Blood and Sand*. I knew I would be OK. How wrong was! I had tears streaming down my face as soon as I saw him, I felt sick in my stomach and basically sobbed. I have turned the TV off now, still in tears. I really hope that Vashti is doing OK. If we are in pieces most of the time, how on earth is she coping?

Andy, I want to wake up and find it's just bad dream, but I can't because it's a painful truth. You are gone from our world, free of pain and whole again. How the angels adore you, as we do, but we cannot smile, not yet. Maybe in time our tears will dry, but not yet.

Love you, Always xx The most beautiful star in the sky!

—Jeannette Smith
Liverpool, England

The first time I saw him in *Spartacus* I was mesmerized. A beautiful man on the outside and a truly beautiful man on the inside. Through this role he inspired many and he will forever be in our hearts and never forgotten.

I hope, Vashti, that you can take strength and comfort from the knowledge that the world grieves with you for the loss of Andy, a husband, a father, a son and an actor. May his broken butterfly wings now be angel wings. Take comfort in knowing that he watches over you and your beautiful children to protect and guide you.

xxx

—Storm
Tewkesbury, England

TRIBUTE

You will always be our Spartacus, now in heaven as our angel and the star that illuminates the path of hope.

—*Alejandra Raggiotti*
Buenos Aires, Argentina

We thought of you with love today,
But that is nothing new.
We thought about you yesterday.
And days before that, too.
We think of you in silence.
We often speak your name.
Now all we have is memories.
And your picture in a frame.
Your memory is our keepsake.
With which we'll never part.
God has you in his keeping.
We have you in our heart.
—Author Unknown

—*Jill 'Dillymoo' Swindell*
Newcastle, UK

My thoughts and prayers go out to you, Vashti, and also to Jesse and Indigo. Andy was a true champion and a mighty warrior. Two qualities that he possessed that made everyone fall in love with him.

Thank you so much for sharing him with the world.

—*Susan Green*
Lancaster, Pennsylvania, USA

Andy Whitfield 1971-2011

Andy you have the face of an angel, the heart of a lion, the body of a god, and you were the most beautiful of men. You will sadly be missed in this earth. You were taken from us—no, stolen from us. Our lives will never be the same ever again.

You will never be replaced. No one could ever stand in your shoes or walk this earth with the same pride and passion and love for people. You were unique Andy, one of a kind. You will be missed for all time.

Love...xxxxx

—Irene
England

To a man who will never be forgotten; a great loss to all of us. Will miss seeing that beautiful face, so much!

Best wishes to Vashti and their beautiful children!

—Karen Flynn
Brittany, France

I'm a cancer survivor, and wanted to tell him he isn't alone. I wished, hoped with all my heart that he would recover. Andy, you're now free of the pain, the fear, the sickness. You are survived by your friends, family and fans and live on in love, and in the short but fantastic career you had!

You once played an angel. Now you are one.

—Aine Lawrence McCormac
Ireland

TRIBUTE

If the people we love are stolen from us..

the way to have them live on

is to never stop loving them..

Real love is forever

Vashti, I can't even imagine how painful it must be for you and your family to lose a man like Andy. I hope you may find some comfort and solace in the wonderful memories and in his legacy, which will live on in each and every one of us.

Andy was one in a million, one in a lifetime. He came into our hearts, into our souls and he didn't go away. We'll never forget him. We'll love him forever because the real love is forever.

—*Paola*
Pescara, Italy

Andy Whitfield 1971-2011

Seasons will change from Summer to Autumn, from Winter to Spring. Lives will change. Loves will change, families will change and we will all get a little older each year. But you will stay as you were: eternally young, eternally loved, eternally serene, eternally in our thoughts, eternally precious.
You were much loved...xxx

—Sandra James
Westlothian, Scotland

Heaven may have gained an angel, but the world lost a true champion.
RIP Andy.

—Michelle
Iowa, USA

You came to life through the love of your parents, and came into this world to succeed, and no doubt, you've done it. Your victory is eternal, is forever! You've lived fast, to go at an early age, but your projects were made. You loved life. You join us together with your great work, your beautiful work, and will live forever with us all in the great memories, in our memory!

Andy, your photos, your work, your person express your beautiful smile, the happiness in your life. Your melodious voice expresses your inner happiness. Your gait says that you were a man well-balanced and surrounded by love. You are a complete human being, beautiful and powerful. You're alive in my memories every day because you're part of my life!

—Lidia E. García
Gran Canaria, Spain

TRIBUTE

Andy, you will be forever in my heart and our hearts, we all miss you so much. Andy Whitfield Forever!

—*Diana Ioana Gheorghe*
Giulianova, Italy

You may be gone, but every emotion you ever had is still around your family and friends, giving them comfort. xxx

—*Sandra James*
Eastcalder, Westlothian, Scotland

When God called Andy home
His angels came to take Andy by the hand
Leading Andy along a shining path
Into a place of Peace and Light.
HOME at last.
Andy saw the Lord open His arms
Welcoming Andy with a huge smile
Into the everlasting Joy and Peace
That is His heart.

We all miss you and love you very much.

—*Jijah Malyaw*
Chicago,USA

Andy Whitfield 1971-2011

You walked your path of life for only a short time, which was filled with love of your wife Vashti and your two truly beautiful children. Some paths are shorter than others and who knows the reasons why? But you succeeded in everything you did and as you were about to reach the pinnacle of your career, it was taken away from you. No answer to that, either.

You were adored by your fans and friends and truly loved by your family and that, in itself, must have given you much comfort.

A broken butterfly now whole again.
Much love,...xx

—*Sandra James*
Westlothian, Scotland

A sweet look...a beautiful smile...you came so fast to my life, to march at the same speed! A voice I need to remember. Andy, a man loved and lost here in the world, you stopped to march to another place. And now, having to go through life without you...

We remember you and we miss you! Tears well up in my eyes for you. It is very sad to continue life, knowing that you're not here!

Always in our hearts!

—*Lidia E. García*
Gran Canaria, Spain

TRIBUTE

Fate hit the heart of us all mercilessly, now we only have the imagination, the imagination to envision what would have been your new gazes, your new smiles and laughter, your new gestures, your new sharing of companionship, love, generosity and passion, your new words spoken in the divine tone of your soft velvet voice. Yes, our imagination, our endless and enduring love, the Legend, the Myth...and the void.

Fate made a mistake.

—Inés
Seville, Spain

There is never an easy way to say goodbye to loved ones. Your cherished last words to your children will be with them forever and the way you described to them what was happening was said with such beauty and love. The family and friends you left behind will forever remember you... a gentle, humorous, loving man.

And Vashti...your best friend and wife. She is forever in everyone's thoughts as are your two beautiful children.

Sleep well, our Hero...

—Sandra James
Westlothian, Scotland

Andy Whitfield 1971-2011

The strength of a man
is not in the width of his shoulders,
it is the size of his arms when they embrace.
The strength of a man
is not in the deepness of his voice,
it is the gentleness used in his words.
The strength of a man
is not in his hair or his chest,
it is in his heart.
The strength of a man
is not in how hard he can hit,
it is in the tenderness of his caresses.
The strength of a man
is not in the women he loved,
it is in being able of truly belong to one woman.
The strength of a man
is not the weight he can lift,
it is the loads that he can bear with serenity.
—Jacqueline M Griffiths

Oh, Andy! You were such a strong man! Forever loved and never forgotten, strong Man and sweet Angel

—Inés
Seville, Spain

Andy...a heart of a naughty boy with a wise mind of an awesome man!
Love you and miss you sooo much, forever.

—Anneke Zelden
The Hague, Netherlands

TRIBUTE

You know everyone thinks Death is a bad thing. It's not. It's the missing part that hurts us. Look at it this way: Heaven is awesome! He just went home, that's all, and we will see him there in Heaven, and we won't know him as down here, but we will know he was Important to us!

RIP Andy!

—*Robert Rowe*
Ramona, California

What strength to train with such vigor, even when the body grew tired! What courage to face the awful diagnosis the first time! What bravery to call the cruel fate of the recurring cancer "another extraordinary journey!" How could anyone not be touched by such grace?

Andy has been my inspiration from day one: to persevere, to try harder, and to endure. And when he was forced to leave *Spartacus*, Andy humbled everyone by being a true champion. When he was forced to leave his physical existence he became a hero to all of us.

Andy Whitfield is an angel who has walked on this Earth.

—*Fulvia Severina*
New York

Thirty-nine years ago, God gave instructions to a beautiful angel, a wonderful angel...You, beautiful Angel! You have to go to Earth and join people around the world. A beautiful world with different languages and races, but without difference in love.

Andy Whitfield 1971-2011

And the sweet Angel became a man for a while. Transformed, he came into the world to feel, breathe, work and love, leaving us all a lasting impression, leaving a trail so great that we cannot forget. An angel on Earth, which will remain forever, until the dawn of time!

Andy Whitfield, you are that Angel, a beautiful man who stole a piece of our hearts, leaving a wonderful inheritance: the ability to continue here with us.

Every day I remember you. Every day I miss you. Every day you come with me. You are the sunlight that illuminates my days. You are the blue sea. I will never forget you as one admirer, one of those many that carry you in their heart: the blue-eyed angel Andy!

—*Lidia E. García*
Gran Canaria, Spain

TRIBUTE

He's the best of the best. His wonderful smile, his voice, attitude, integrity, attitude, honesty, charisma, and personality conquered the entire world. He left us so early and he left a space no one can replace. It is very unfair, his death.

I miss him so, so, so much.

—*Lavinia Goretti Carmona*
Lisbon, Portugal

The truest words of all: I will not forget you.
You are in my waking thoughts,
*   my sweetest memories, my dearest dreams.*
I will not forget you.
You have touched my soul, opened my eyes,
changed my very experience of the universe.
I will not forget you.
I see you in the flowers, the sunset,
the sweep of the horizon
and all things that stretch to infinity.
I will not forget you.
I have carved you on the palm of my hand.
I carry you with me forever.
    —Ellen Sue Stern, *Living with Loss*, 1995

I found this and I think this is how we all feel about Andy. A few more tears fell... xxx

—*Jeannette Smith*
Liverpool, England

Andy Whitfield 1971-2011

Dear Vashti, Jesse and Indigo,

I wanted to write and tell you how sorry I am for your loss.

May it comfort you to know that so many people care and are thinking of you and your family at this time. Andy was such a beautiful man with a golden heart. So many people will miss him. As a fan I will always keep your family close to my heart and in my prayers.

Andy brought so much pleasure to everyone he met and even to those who he never met, and will be sadly missed. He came into our lives through television and film and we couldn't help but fall in love with such a beautiful man. He made us laugh and cry and gave us so much pleasure as we watched his career unfold on our screens, and when we heard that our brave warrior had lost his fight, tears fell and a void was left in our hearts.

There are no words to describe how much we love Andy.

He was a loving husband and doting father and will always be watching over you. I pray every day to give you strength when you need it most.

May the love of family and friends comfort you.

With love and sympathy

—*Jill "Dillymoo" Swindell*
Newcastle, UK

TRIBUTE

A Hero doesn't need to always win the battle, a Hero is the man who, throughout his life and in extraordinary and more difficult times, did what he could with grace and dignity, as you truly did, my brave warrior. Nothing will keep me from returning to your memories, not the pain nor the sadness nor time itself.

Forever in my heart.

—*Inés*
Seville, Spain

I'll Be Seeing You

I'll be seeing you
Hey don't forget your coat
I'll be seeing you
Feels like it's turning cold
I hate that you're leaving
With so much unsaid and
This strange empty feeling
Won't let me forget
That I'll be seeing you
I'll be seeing you
Oh, that beautiful smile
I'll be seeing you
Sure as I'm seeing you now.
Around every corner
Wherever I go
Every moment of everyday
Darling I know

Andy Whitfield 1971-2011

That I'll be seeing you.
I'll be seeing you
Oh the nights I've cried
But maybe, just maybe
In time, I'll be fine.
I'll be seeing you
When I close my eyes
I'll be seeing you
I've got you memorized.
I'll always love you
I know you know that.
And I know that in my heart,
That you're not coming back
But in everything I do…
I'll be seeing you.
                    —Cindi Thomson

—*Jeannette Smith*
Liverpool, England

Words are not enough to express the loss…the words are a small part of our pain. Our hearts have been broken into pieces. My heart is enveloped by the sadness and pain…empty handed…tears for you… Time does not heal wounds, but the passage of time will help!

A handsome man, a great husband,a wonderful father,a fantastic actor: Andy Whitfield. The memory of you is not enough. We all love you here, but we are still thinking, why?

Now my journey through life is different because I cannot stop thinking about you! Unconditional Love !

—*Lidia E. García*
Gran Canaria, Spain

TRIBUTE

To Vashti Whitfield,

Sending warm caring thoughts around your broken heart to keep it safe until you're strong again.
Hugs to Jesse Red and Indigo Sky.

—Jijah Malyaw
Chicago, USA

Responding to a Facebook post I realized how much an open heart will affect this world...a small ripple that spreads everywhere. I'm re-posting part of my response for Vashti to read so she can know that her husband and the father of her children, although taken too soon, remains a force for so many here. A small comfort, I know, but one I hope will give her a little lift.

You are alive and sane to feel this way. We all do here. And the fact is that Andy Whitfield put so much humanity into his performances, which means we all "felt" right along with him, so to lose even that connection is painful, so much more for those who knew him as a man and for Vashti and their children who knew him as their family.

Hug your family and friends, tell them you love them and a small part of Andy will remain here with us all!

—Elizabeth Biggerstaff
Delmar, New York

Andy Whitfield 1971-2011

Every once in a while a stranger enters our lives and heart for whatever reason, just long enough to change and touch us and make an impact on our lives while also becoming a friend. Andy was that for me.

Ironically, most of us probably have a lot of friends that we don't truly know all that well if we really were to analyze it: siblings, parents, other relatives that we see often. We ask ourselves "who are they really?" So, when you think about it, it isn't so unfathomable to grow to greatly love a man we've never met, spoken to, hugged, or even shaken hands with. We welcomed him into our homes weekly, with much enthusiasm and open arms. What began as pure entertainment transformed into pure love, admiration and a deep sense of loss.

He literally dropped into my life one wintry January morning. He left almost as quickly, but not before making an indelible mark on my soul and heart. It kind of makes no sense to many, but *c'est la vie.*

He left only AFTER he completely touched me and filled me with admiration, love, inspiration, and respect. The pain he suffered for eighteen months has somehow now become our pain to bear in his passing, one I am proud to own, knowing he is now pain-free.

It will ease, in time, and his memory and his grace will shine not only in our hearts, but in the hearts of his children and the wife he left behind. Andy gave us a real gift: the gift of knowing him in the only ways we could. But, he made us care...just by being himself.

Andy, we will miss you so very very much and your beauty, smiles and grace are forever ingrained on our hearts, etched into our souls. It is my hope that this tribute can somehow let you and your lovely, sweet family know just how truly loved and respected you are, and maybe let your family know they are certainly never alone. A legion of fans are out there praying for them and holding them close in their hearts.

Thank you Andy for blessing and enriching our lives with your smiles, performances, and your life. Thank you Vashti for being such a supportive and loving wife and sharing him with us. We will always cherish and love The Whitfields, our little extended family in Australia.

May God find little and lovely ways to comfort you in this difficult time.

—Terri Fentress
Bowling Green, Kentucky, USA

A beautiful shade, a shining star and its nice light, the blue sky, the most beautiful smile, the sun and its brightness—thousands of hearts, give love. Do not forget: feel surrounded by the love we send you! I pray for you, I write for you, I weep for you. You are not, but it seems you're still here. I don't want to forget, I refuse to forget, because my love for you is forever.

I miss you! My Angel Andy!

—Lidia E. García
Gran Canaria, Spain

As told by another...You embraced your fate. But how I wish life could have embraced you.
Much love...xxx

—Sandra James
Scotland

Andy Whitfield 1971-2011

His voice is something from another world—strong, resonant, beautiful, full, melodious, hot, sweet, wonderful—captivating all of us who were involved immediately, at the first second, even. The voice of an angel. I miss him.

—*Lavinia Goretti Carmona*
Lisbon, Portugal

You will be in my memory forever sweet angel...

—*Edyta Burda*
Libiaz, Poland

Since the death of Andy I'm feeling like a different person and I cannot explain. I feel anger so great and at the same time I'm thinking about going to do volunteer work. I always thought to do it, but now I feel something pushes me to help others.

When I go on the street, I always go with headphones just to get removed from all that noise around me. Andy changed my life. He gave us a huge force that changed many of us...

—*Lavinia Goretti Carmona*
Lisbon, Portugal

TRIBUTE

Andy, a man...the actor...a son, a father and a loving husband...you left without saying goodbye to us. You lived your last days surrounded by the love of your family. That was the most important thing, but your death came as a surprise. It shocked us. We all lived in prayer for your recovery. Your illness brought us together in a big family with love for you, but the worst happened, the bad news came and broke my heart and now I mourn your loss. We're heartbroken in this world.

Time does not heal the wounds, time only helps to continue living. Your smile...your voice...your eyes...your face...your work...everything is here with peace of mind knowing that you are not going to suffer any more. But our tears do not stop, every day they flow for you!

I miss you and it is difficult to continue here without ever seeing your great smile!

—*Lidia E. García*
Gran Canaria, Spain

Death is Nothing.

I only passed on the other side of the road.
I am me, you are you; what I was for you, I'll still be.
Give me the name you always gave me,
talk to meas you have always done.
You continue to live in the world of creatures,
I'm living in the world of the Creator.
Do not use a tone solemn or sad,
continue to laugh about what made us laugh together,

Andy Whitfield 1971-2011

Pray, smile, think of me, Pray for me.
My name shall be pronounced as always,
without emphasis of any kind,
without a trace of shadow or sadness.
Life means all that it always meant,
the cord was not cut.
Why would I be out of their thoughts
now that I'm just out of their lives?
I'm not far I'm just on the other side of the road...
You who are there, go forward, life goes on,
amazing and beautiful as ever...
— St. Augustine

Andy will never be forgotten by the world. He was special and went to heaven. We pray for him and we miss him a lot.

—Lavinia Goretti Carmona
Lisbon, Portugal

The first time I ever saw Andy was a few years ago in the movie *Gabriel*. There was something about him that just captured me. His soul just shone right through the screen. I was mesmerized by him. I always wondered where he had gone.

Then, one day, I was flipping through the channels, and caught a glimpse of this gladiator that looked a lot like that guy, Andy Whitfield, from the movie *Gabriel*. I was so excited to see him again! Once again, I was fascinated,

TRIBUTE

mesmerized, captured by his brilliance, his talent, his emotion, his passion. I began watching *Spartacus Blood and Sand*. What a brilliant series!

I was floored. I looked forward to every Sunday to see the next episode.

Last fall, October 2010, I lost my dad, whose name was also Andy. I was devastated. Then, I heard about Andy having to back out of *Spartacus* to start aggressive treatment. So, I thought, why not check and see if there is a fan page on Facebook for him? I did, and found an amazing page full of beautiful, loving people. I have since become close to nine specific women. We came together for the love of one man, Mr. Andy Whitfield. These ladies helped me through the loss of my dad, they were an absolute blessing. I will always thank Andy for bringing them into my life.

Vashti, Indigo, and Jesse, please know that my love for Andy passes on to you as well. You are always in my thoughts and prayers. You are always in my heart. I cannot imagine the pain of losing a husband, or father at such a young age. I was at least an adult when I lost my dad, and the pain was almost unbearable. Just know, that I am always thinking of you.

Andy, you were an amazing man, father, husband, friend and cast mate. I know this because of the interviews with your family and friends, as well as interviews of you. Your soul shone through your eyes...and captured us all. So, our beautiful butterfly, rest peacefully, no more pain, until we all meet again.

Love you much...miss you more. I will never forget you, Andy.

All my Love,

—*Natasha Caverly Brooks*
Alberta, Canada

Andy Whitfield 1971-2011

I loved watching Andy. Anytime I was depressed I would put in one of his movies and just his smile would make me feel better. To see the kindness, love, and caring in his eyes would let you know that there are true Angels among us. Andy was my Angel in the darkness. I would like to thank Vashti for helping Andy touch all of our lives. God Bless you Vashti and your children.

Will miss you always Andy Whitfield—my true Gabriel!

—Vicki Farine
Siloam Springs, Arkansas, USA

I always knew Andy was an amazing man and he drew incredible people to him like a magnet. The proof of this is in his fans. The great man is gone now but his amazing fans still rally to his cause. The man had a way about him that brought the best out in people all over our planet, and even though he is no longer with us, the goodness he inspired in all of us is still so evident in every word I read from all of you wonderful people that still band together to do good for Andy's family and fans. Andy, you are gone now, but your goodness remains. Your fans are incredible people.

Hugs to you all! Cheers to you, Andy, we miss you so.
A friend and great admirer...

—Danny Miller
Canada

TRIBUTE

Dear Vashti,

I just wanted to thank you for sharing your wonderful gift of a husband with the world. I want you to know how sorry I am for your loss and to know that your loss is our loss.

The world didn't get to see what we all knew Andy was about to achieve, the greatness that was within him, the greatness that we were waiting for until we heard the news of his untimely passing. God now has our beautiful butterfly angel, but I know he walks beside you and your children every day and night.

Be strong and let all of your beautiful memories comfort you, and know that Andy's fans will always be here and that he will never ever be forgotten.

God Bless you and your family, and Andy's parents and his sister. This is my tribute to a beautiful soul, the one that I call our Beautiful Butterfly Angel.

With much love,

—*Trina Aguilar*
Norwalk, Connecticut, USA

A beautiful smile...an amazing face...a voice...the true expression...a great heart...I still wonder why... Vashti, you share the sadness and loneliness. And I would give you a hug to share, honest with tears. Jesse and Indigo, my prayers are with you always. We all remember your dad! Andy Whitfield...from the other side, give us the strength to continue, because it's very hard. Now you're in peace!

—*Lidia E. García*
Gran Canaria, Spain

Andy Whitfield 1971-2011

TRIBUTE

May you find comfort in the beautiful memories your loving husband gave you and your children, Vashti, during your time of sorrow.

Andy's immeasurable courage has inspired and touched the lives of so many. No words can ever express the deep sense of loss to a wife and child, no thought or prayer can take away the pain. Just know that his fans and those his own personal story has touched wish you, your children and his family our very best in your time of need.

—*Pam Stewart*
Sturbridge, Massachusetts, USA

Behind the crying is the silence, behind the silence is the memory and behind remembrance, the moments. We are like birds that must migrate or like stones that must keep rolling. After a final farewell, life always continues.

—Alessandro Mazariegos

Vashti,

I cannot imagine the magnitude of the ordeal you are going through, facing life without him by your side,but just think that, in spite of the unbearable pain of his loss, it is preferable to have had a short time by the side of such a wonderful, gentle, strong, beautiful and extraordinary man than a whole life without having known him.

All my love for you, your beautiful children, and for his parents. No parent should have to outlive their children.

—*Inés*
Seville, Spain

Andy Whitfield 1971-2011

It has taken me too long to contribute to this wonderful tribute book, words still fail me, and I cannot help the tears welling in my eyes as I write this. I guess I haven't yet wrapped my mind around our loss, and I don't think I ever will, but then again, I want him to know how much he still means, and will forever mean to me.

Since the very first moment I saw him on screen, Andy touched my very heart. It was his warmth, his tenderness, his closeness, his presence, his soul. It was him. Just him. I could go on for pages and pages just naming all of his qualities and features that caught my heart.

His eyes, the bluest and sweetest I have ever seen. Just with one look of those blue eyes, deep and wide as the ocean, you could see right through them and into his very soul. He was able to convey the strongest of emotions. He could make you relate to him, make you go mad with rage, melt down, burn up with desire, and shatter with his pain.

His bright, ear-to-ear smile, and that naughty grin that used to make me giggle every time I saw it, now make me just crave for him to come back to us.

His voice, deep, soft, however powerful and strong. At times it sounded like a whisper, but still it managed to make my heart flutter in my chest.

But, above all that, his persona. His heart. His soul. He could make everyone better just for knowing him, and by extension—even though I never had the pleasure of meeting him—he sure made me a much better person.

He became my inspiration, my reason to do what I love doing most, and to this day, I have to say that I had never found anyone who could provoke so many feelings brewing up inside of me the way he did, and still does.

TRIBUTE

The world is by far a much a lesser place now without his cleansing light, and I shall forever keep him in my heart. All my love, best wishes and upmost respect to his loving family.

—*Beatriz Suarez Diez "Ladarkfemme"*
Spain

My darling Andy, a beautiful Angel, blue eyes looking down from the heavens! I miss you so much, we need you; all of us need you! Many beautiful images of you...right now in paradise...in the distance...and forever. So sad and so hard,
Life is difficult without you, Andy Whitfield!

—*Lidia E. García*
Gran Canaria, Spain

Hello my dear Vashti, my beautiful and brave young lady, I think of you so often it's like I know you. I so wish that I could give you and your babies the biggest hugs, to reassure you, to tell you everything's going to be all right, but I don't know how. It still feels so raw, but I want you to know that we all send our love your way.

You are always in my thoughts, my prayers are with you all and will be for a long long time. Love and respect to you.

Love xxxxxx,

—*Irene*
London

Andy Whitfield 1971-2011

I will remember and never forget! No words can express what I feel, or what I felt when I've heard that Andy passed away. My heart stopped and part of it died with him. Tears flowed down my cheeks and I could not breathe. We lost someone very important, no one and nothing will be able to replace him.

Andy, you were one in a million. Your captivating smile and hypnotic blue eyes are still hard to look away from. Still don't believe it—someone made a big mistake. We feel your absence! Until the last moment we lived hoping that we would see you again, that the great warrior Spartacus would return to the arena. You are not here anymore, no longer— sadness, anger, sorrow, this is what I feel.

I am very sorry that your beloved wife and children are alone, without loving husband and daddy. The pain of losing someone so wonderful is impossible to relieve, to soothe. Vashti, Jesse Red and Indigo Sky—I'm thinking of you every day. I hope that our meeting will be one day in heaven.

I miss you all the time. Remembering...

—Kaska Bugajska
Poland

It was a gift to have you grace us with your presence, if only for so short a time. Thank you for touching our lives so deeply. You will live on eternally in our hearts.

R.I.P. our dear Andy

—Terri Fentress
Bowling Green, Kentucky, USA

TRIBUTE

Andy, you left the world in pain and crying for you. You were a hidden treasure, but soon you took possession of us all. They could explain your disease, but not your death. So sudden, so fast. I cannot accept it. They can say they did all they could, but they were not able to have you cured. They did not save you.

You did not need to make more movies to show your value to the world, or to prove what a wonderful man you were: the best of all.

The physical effort the role demanded has been too painful, they pushed you a lot and it did not help you.

We just wanted you here, not where you are now. Here was your space. I think that you didn't go away, but that you are sleeping, to rest close to us.

I don't want to, nor can I accept that you left.

—*Lavinia Goretti Carmona*
Lisbon, Portugal

He created a strong bond, a link so big and strong that we cannot break it. He took possession of our hearts, completely stole our hearts, and left with his hands full of love, but leaving our empty lives to mourn their loss. Our chest no longer feels happiness, everyday giving us the sad reality of sorrow and tears. I do not understand.

I did not get to know him personally, but this man has changed my life forever, and now I cannot help but feel immense sadness for the loss.

I don't like my life. Today it has rained in the Canary Islands, and the punishment is even deeper.

I miss you, Sweet Angel Blue Eyes! Our beloved Andy!

—*Lidia E. García*
Gran Canaria, Spain

Andy Whitfield 1971-2011

Dearest Vashti,

I feel Andy's loss very keenly and it is very hard to overcome the fact that someone like him is not here anymore, but I'm sure his soul will always be by your side and with the children. It will be the angelic butterfly that stays with each of you. Andy was very happy and in heaven there is a smiling star who will remember this forever. Be strong and move forward
I will never forget you, Andy Whitfield.

—Aldana Cereto, 16 years old
Temperley, Buenos Aires, Argentina

Thoughts of you forever on our minds, you are safe now, comforted in the arms of your loved ones who have gone before you.
Much love...xxx

—Sandra James
Scotland

Dear Vashti and family,

So shocked to hear the sad news of Andy's passing. Andy was a great actor, and I loved him in *Spartacus*. Andy came across as a very humble and down to earth person, so lovely. He would have gone on to great and bigger things if he had been given the chance.
RIP Andy.

—Shirley Kirkaldy
Scotland, United Kingdom

TRIBUTE

Where the sun is high and the air is sweet, with open arms Vashti will run to you, her warrior so brave and strong For now you need this rest after fighting for so long You'll never be forgotten nor unloved.

So go to sleep, sweet butterfly Spread your wings up to the sky.

—*Abir Mansur*
Sweden

Was Andy Whitfield really only a man?

When Andy roared on the scene as *Spartacus* in 2009, I was enraptured by his mesmerizing performance, by his utter gorgeousness and that charismatic blue gaze that could melt steel or dissolve into sweet tenderness.

What talent! Such strength! Such passion! And that voice—nobody else can even come close...

Moreover, Andy was said to be the funniest, kindest, easiest to work with and down-to-earth leading man, ever!

He instantly became my greatest inspiration to push myself harder, to achieve more, and to become the best that I can be. And when I heard that he was fighting his own personal battle with so much quiet bravery, and could even see the positive in such an ordeal, I was humbled by his courage and grace. I was overjoyed when we were told that Andy had been victorious in summer of 2010 and then was devastated only a few months after.

Who can call such a cruel fate "another extraordinary

journey"? What superhuman inner strength did Andy possess? Was it the support of his wonderful wife and sweet children? Or was it the expression of something divine?

Andy is unlike anybody I have ever met or heard of. How can a complete stranger have such an impact on so many people? How could he touch our very souls and leave such an imprint on our hearts that it hurts so much to know he is no longer with us?

Every day I think of him. I think of you, Vashti, and your children. I wish it could be undone, I wish Andy could prove to the world that he is the greatest champion there ever was, an extraordinary human being, a loving husband and father, a true hero or more.

Andy Whitfield is an Angel who walked on this Earth for too short a time, but he left a legacy that will endure forever.

—*Irena*
New York

A great soul serves everyone all the time.
A great soul never dies.
It brings us together again & again...
—Maya Angelou

That is our angel Andy.

—*Jijah Malyaw*
Chicago, USA

TRIBUTE

They say there is a reason
They say that time will heal
But neither time nor reason
Will change the way we feel
For no one knows the heartache
That lies behind our smiles
No one knows how many times
We have broken down and cried.
We want to tell you something
So there won't be any doubt
You're so wonderful to think of
But so hard to be without...
　　　　　　—Author Unknown

—Kim Minniti
Pawling, New York

You left this world without saying goodbye, leaving an immense gap in the hearts of many people.

Today, from where you are, be it that heaven is your eternal home; death is like that, beautiful, magical, ephemeral. Your smile will be the ideal company for God, your joy the key to paradise, your face the light that illuminates the darkness.

Rest in peace in the middle of jasmine, carnations, and roses, waiting for us to keep you company. Enjoy your stay, surrounded by angels, snow-white clouds and the unmatched company of the Almighty. Someday soon we'll all be together.

—Alejandra Raggiotti
Buenos Aires, Argentina

Andy Whitfield 1971-2011

Andy Whitfield. Your look expresses truth, your blue eyes offer reality. Demonstrate the way you walk in peace, now in the heavens. Your way through life has not been indifferent, you're still here, with my breathing and my feelings for you because you live in my thoughts. You live in me!

My heart beats in my chest, and part of my heart belongs to you. My journey through life is important, and part of my life is you, because you're alive in my memory.

Your physical part has left this world, and that's what makes us suffer more, but your spiritual being, your inner beauty is here with us all.

You were a good friend. Now, when your friends remember you, they're friends at heart. You were a wonderful actor, and all your fans miss you.

From Lidia, a true fan, one more person. And although I have not met you personally, I am a person missing a piece of my heart! Thank you!

—Lidia E. García
Gran Canaria, Spain

Hi Vashti,

I'm sending some love your way with a big hug for you and the babies...please feel my arms around you giving you my biggest bear hugs. I want to comfort you all...to offer you something that might ease your pain...a kind word, a gentle touch, to hold your hand...I wish I could do these things for you...my brave strong lady...love and respect to you...xxxxxx

—Irene
London

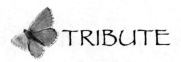# TRIBUTE

Como un rayo de luz entraste en nuestras vidas y una estela brillante dejaste en nuestros corazones. Nuestros corazones heridos en estos momentos pueden continuar simplemente porque tu llama siempre esta presente y arde dentro de nosotros. Eres una estrella que brilla mucho mas alla del firmamento, nos ilumina cada noche y guia dia a dia para que nunca te olvidemos y nunca lo haremos. Por siempre estaras en nuestras vidas y nuestros corazones.
Encuentra tu paz angelito
.

Translation:

Like a ray of light you came into our lives and left a bright trail in our hearts. Our wounded hearts can continue right now simply because your flame is always present and burns within us. You're a star that shines far beyond the sky, illuminates every night for us and guides us day to day so we will never forget you and we never will. Forever you will be in our lives and our hearts. Find your peace angel.

—Elizabeth Segarra
Spain

Andy, you made the difference between GOOD and BAD. You were the difference that we needed to look inside ourselves, for us to see what in the world is good or not, and you were GOOD. You were the smile that was missing in all of us. With you, we learned to suffer, fight, laugh, but didn't learn to lose you. With you, we learned to smile even while suffering. You were the rainbow everyone is seeking, but unfortunately left us so early. You left, having touched our lives forever. The light, words emanating from your eyes,

Andy Whitfield 1971-2011

yes, because your gaze spoke, said it all, the man you were, all of you was something unusual, exceptional, different. Now, your absence destroys us emotionally, it devastated us and changed us, changed me. How can I watch TV, movies, etc, if you don't appear anymore?

Who were you, Andy Whitfield, that you touched the entire world? What strength came from you that embraced us all and with your death we are devastated? What gift did you have to eclipse many well known actors and actresses? Everything that came from you was charming, wonderful and "infected" us forever. Your passage was so short, but your legacy left your mark on our soul.

What world is this? What is beyond death? Where are you? You are alone and we need you here. The days pass away, but are darker without you, because you took the light with you.

You made me think that life is nothing. I still feel many miss you. Oh, Andy, we miss you; I miss you so much! I'm always praying for you

—*Lavinia Goretti Carmona*
Lisbon, Portugal

What we have once enjoyed we can never lose. All that we love deeply becomes a part of us.

Andy, we will love and miss you for eternity. We will see you again, our beautiful butterfly, our Champion xxx

—*Jeannette Smith*
Liverpool, UK

TRIBUTE

For Andy and Vashti,

I read from your eyes that you should go. I was afraid of The Day, and my heart was screaming, "Come back!" Your light, my anger, your fear, my singing.

Hand in hand straight ahead—this is all that I want. Wake me up with your kiss...Let it be over, that bad dream about the future. I open my sad eyes—because my world is dying. Loveless, your love missing. This entire world weakens, when the love is ending. It's only YOU who has this power. Please wake me up, and save him!

—*Kaska Bugajska*
Poland

Your story will always be one of inspiration, and bravery, leaving your home to create a new life, succeeding in all you do, never giving up, never complaining, embracing all of life's challenges, giving your family and all those who hold you close your all. Holding your head up high and yet remaining humble and understated. I know you never wanted to be a hero, but if you could see what we see, you would understand why all of your fans love you the way we do. Your spirit burns bright, your talent is evident, and you will never be forgotten. I wish nothing but love and happiness to all those close to you, I hope the love of your fans extends to them and gives comfort to them as they reel from the shock of losing you.

You will always be a star burning bright, lighting the way. You gave far more than you will ever realize. Peace, love and my deepest condolences to your beautiful family.

—*Caz*
Wolverhampton, England

Andy Whitfield 1971-2011

Not only did Andy have an impact on the lives of adults, but children as well. My middle son, Connor, admired Andy so much; he would wear mock-up costumes pretending to be Andy. Running around with sword and shield, he was every bit a young Spartacus. Andy you had an impact on us, young and old. You were such a true hero!

—Danny Miller
a friend and great admirer from Canada

Andy, you were a brave warrior and such a good man. When I am older I want to get a tattoo that says Andy Whitfield *Blood and Sand*. I really liked your show and I think you were the best Spartacus. I used to sneak from my room at night to watch you battle; then my mom and dad would catch me and send me back to bed. I am really sorry you are gone and now I miss you soooo much.
Love...

—Connor Miller, 8 years old
Canada

This Saturday night I saw the final chapter of *Blood and Sand* again and I realized something: Andy won his fight against his illness even before he knew about it, because with his interpretation in this show, he will live forever! He is immortal in his amazing work!

Thanks, Andy!

—Carlos Galvez
Rosario, Argentina

TRIBUTE

To me, there are many brilliant actors and many wonderful performances and Andy's Spartacus is up there with all of them. The tragedy is that unlike those other brilliant actors, Andy is not around to show all the many brilliant performances that were in him. It is our great loss. But the actor and the man have affected and inspired me in a very unique way. To me, I will always remember him as a Beautiful Warrior. To quote a Seal song, he "burns in me like a shining star."

—*Kate Pak*
Teaneck, New Jersey, USA

Why your graceful and stunning presence in this world has been denied to us all is something that I will never understand...I see you, and every time I confirm that you are the only one who is able, before and after, to make me experience this "satisfaction" of my senses and my spirit, which keeps me unable to spend a day without you...words really cannot describe the need for you...

—*Inés*
Spain

He flew to the sky...my heart is broken and lives in pain...and I miss you so much, my heart is broken and lives in pain...and your images are there...I see you...but my heart is broken and lives in pain...I had not in my power the miracle to give health...give life...tears and sadness...life goes on, and you're not here! Andy Whitfield!

—*Lidia E. García*
Gran Canaria, Spain

Andy Whitfield 1971-2011

Hay personas que pasan por este mundo desapercibidas y las hay, como es el caso de Andy, que su paso estaba predestinado a llegar al corazon de todos, seguro que ha sido por algun bien, necesitabamos a alguien positivo como el, solo que nos lo hayan arrebatado tan pronto nos ha dejado tal dolor emocional que ahora, el mundo es un poco mas triste...

Translation:

There are people who go through this world unnoticed and there are those, as is the case with Andy, that his journey was destined to reach the hearts of all. He has surely been here for something good, we needed someone as positive; only that he was taken from us so soon, which has left such emotional pain that now the world is a little sadder...

—Elizabeth Segarra
Spain

I understand that this is more difficult for you and the kids, we pray that God gives you strength and courage to move on. We love Andy & we love his family too. God Bless!

—Lotis B. Mendoza
Jacksonville, Florida USA

TRIBUTE

Dear Vashti and family,

I wish you all the best for the future. Andy was a great person and actor. He was a fighter. When I heard he passed away I was so sad and could not believe it. Still can't. Andy has a special place forever in my heart. We will never forget him.

—Hannelore Kurzke
Bielefeld, Germany

Although our hearts are broken and we grieve for Andy's family and ourselves, and as much as we do not want to accept it, just the shell of the man is gone. Andy lives on in our hearts and in the celestial realm where we will all meet again.
I am still so sad, so sad.

—Linda Joines Wimert

Baltimore, Maryland, USA

My friend, you now walk alongside God as his newest warrior angel. There is no doubt the Kingdom of Heaven is more beautiful than ever before, because heaven now has the most beautiful soul ever that has graced our world

—Danny Miller
a friend and great admirer from Canada

Andy Whitfield 1971-2011

TRIBUTE

He was a master at conveying his emotions through his eyes and his facial expressions...there is not one still picture from the show that does not demonstrate this. You can look at any photo and know exactly what his character was feeling in that moment. He was brilliant! Definitely one of the best actors I have ever known

—*Jodi Moyer Lane*
Colborne, Ontario, Canada

Very close, but so far away...look at the sky!
We live our lives...walk and feel!
Feelings...memories and breath!
Words and I wonder, why?
Staying with us for little time,
to go to heaven very soon...OMG.
But nothing else matters...An Angel!
We open our mind to get to you, thanks to spirituality!
You are here...You're always up here with us!
You're here, Andy Whitfield!

—*Lidia E. García*
Gran Canaria, Spain

I first saw Andy in *Gabriel* and was blown away by his sweetness and power...I read that he was very choosy about his projects so although I looked for him, I didn't see him until *Spartacus* and was so thrilled by the series and his performance. When I first heard he had been diagnosed with

Andy Whitfield 1971-2011

Non Hodgkin's Lymphoma I thought "#@! that is a bad disease" and I worried, but all I read from him and his reps was so positive that I believed, unreservedly, he would beat it against the odds...

I really just believed, even though I've seen what cancer can do to a human body...when he passed I was in shock, just numb with disbelief and grief, and although I have a strong belief in a beautiful loving God, I will never understand, at least not until I'm on the other side where I think we'll be given the answers.

Our world is less than it was when Andy was here, but we are blessed to have had him for the time we did. Blessings to his family...I hope they get that wonderful feeling of being visited by a loved one, I know he holds them in his arms all the time...

—Elizabeth Biggerstaff
Delmar, New York

11-11-11...My heart is broken again, again, again... without you there isn't any more happiness in me...you are my first thought of the day...and every day I look up at the sky and smile because I know...you are there...

I'll miss you forever, Andy.

Honor and Glory and all my love.

—Marina
Italy

TRIBUTE

I would like to wish Vashti and the children a lot of strength and only the best in their whole lives.

Andy was a man who affected a lot of people around the world and therefore still lives in the hearts of us all. My dad died twenty-five years ago, a man who gave a lot to me—in fact, is still with me in my heart. Andy will be there for you and the children as well.

—*Alex Vlachová*
Prague, Czech Republic

Dearest Vashti & family,

I never admired any person or actor the way I do Andy. Even now, my heart is still aching every time I see a photo or a video of him and know that I will never see more of him. I feel like I lost someone from my own family.

I got to know him when my husband encouraged me to watch *Spartacus*, because I don't usually watch brutal shows, but I just started liking his character as a Gladiator and fell in love with him more when I researched his personal life; how humble and great an actor he was, and I was saddened when I found out about his illness. I'm one of those who actually prayed for his recovery. I guess I didn't pray hard enough.

I understand that this is more difficult for you and the kids, we pray that God gives you strength and courage to move on. We love Andy & we love his family too. God Bless!

—*Lotis B. Mendoza*
acksonville, Florida USA

Andy Whitfield 1971-2011

Andy, I'm sitting here looking at your photo...you are speaking to me with your eyes; your telling me it's OK, I'm OK, don't worry I'm fine; it's just so hard even now. Seven weeks have passed...it seems like yesterday...I'm still so sad, so heartbroken. I think of Vashti, Jesse and Indi every day, hoping and praying that they're OK. I'm so glad that I have so many beautiful friends to help me through...thanks to you...you will always be my shining light, my inspiration, my hero my champion...I miss you so much...I love you so much...love...xxxxxx

—*Irene*
London

Caro Andy,

Hai trasmesso attraverso la tua anima il senso dell' amicizia, del rispetto, dell'amore, il senso della dignità, dell' umanità (non facile oggi) ma Tu sei arrivato...anche se attraverso una televisione, e le cose si sono fermate... fermate per riflettere e avere tempo per amare di nuovo il mondo, l'amore.

Ringraziamo chi Ti ha scelto per trasmettere a tutti noi la Tua semplicità di UOMO. Grazie—grazie a tutti Ti ricorderemo sempre con affetto e stima.

Translation:

Dear Andy,

Through your soul you have conveyed the essence of friendship, respect, love, a sense of dignity, of humanity (not easy today), but you have succeeded...even if it was across

TRIBUTE

television, and things have stopped...stopped to reflect and have time to be fond of the world and love again. We thank him who chose YOU to express to us all your simplicity of MAN. Thanks—thanks to all. We will always remember you with affection and respect.

—*Maddalena e famiglia*
Milano, Italy

Good morning, sweet Angel of Light...Andy Whitfield: Every day we're feeling close to you, closer to your huge heart, the heart of love for your wife Vashti, and your little treasures, Jesse and Indigo. Your loving wife lets all of us be part of your family...Vashti is a wonderful woman, and your children are beautiful.

I miss you, I miss you so much, but I just think of your family, Vashti and the kids; they're fighting for happiness every day, and it changes my mood...I'm bound to feel happiness too!

You know, Andy, I started to watch the continuation of your series on the network, with Liam, and I had to stop watching it...My heart broke for grief and sorrow...but you gave your blessing...you loved the show so much...you wanted the series to continue without you, and I'm proud of your person...You're the best!

You—man, actor, husband and father, you have achieved a better world, a world of love and unity, your fans mourn and love you every day...I'll take you in my heart...Thanks!

—*Lidia E. García*
Gran Canaria, Spain

Andy Whitfield 1971-2011

Time passes but, Andy, I still can't believe you're gone, it seems like a bad dream I'm still hoping I'll wake up and it's been a bad dream...and then I realize it's true and the tears fall...I light candles again today for you in your honor, in remembrance...you will remain in my heart forever ...because that's where you belong, my champion my hero...love as always for you

My love and respect to beautiful Vashti, Jesse and Indigo...they too remain in my heart I pray for peace and encouragement for them. Big hugs to you... xxxxxx

—Irene
London

I never met you; didn't know you were sick until the very day you died, but the feeling that maybe, if one more heart prayed to God, maybe you could have survived and we would get to see you longer on the screen in our hearts. That was not so, because God found a better place for you in the sky where you are pain free. You changed parts of my life and expectations, hopes. You are my hero, you make me want to look for better things. I cried for you like I never cried for family members, to this day I have music on my phone that makes me think of you and suddenly I erupt in tears. Vashti is a strong, yet very lucky woman to have had you in her life. For today and the rest of my life, Andy Whitfield, I will forever miss you; only an act of God can make me forget you. I Love You!

You Are *The Wind Beneath My Wings* Hero.

—Isha Moore
Carenage, Trinidad

TRIBUTE

As huge Spartacus fans we were deeply saddened by Andy's untimely passing. We always thought that he'd pull through because Andy was Spartacus and Spartacus never lost a fight. It's tragic and unfortunate that he lost the biggest battle of his life and his kids won't get to know him, but when Jesse and baby girl Indigo Sky are a little older they can watch the show and see how strong and invincible their dad once was.

Andy will always have a special place in our hearts. Much love,

—Zeynep & Elif Erol
Istanbul, Turkey

We wish we could hear you say, "I am Spartacus!" once again, but instead you're in Heaven, playing in God's arena, showing off your amazing talent to the other Angels ~Winks~ And we're here missing you every minute, praying for the strength to carry on your name and legend, which we will, especially with the help of your beloved wife Vashti. Some people believe that Angels exist...I KNOW they do, because Andy is watching over Vashti, Jesse, Indigo and us everyday.

—Patti T.
USA

Andy Whitfield 1971-2011

For Vashti...

Every time I think of Vashti, my heart is breaking into pieces but I also think...she is very lucky; much more than many people in this life, she had the opportunity to meet the most wonderful man who has ever walked this earth, lived for seven years in a perfect relationship and has two beautiful children that every time she looks at them she'll see their father reflected in them. Vashti. It is very difficult to find true love in this life and losing it is even harder. Andy was a devoted husband, loving father and true friend I know, but be strong and safe for your children please, because Andy is taking care of you and he is smiling to have the best wonderful family in this world. Andy will always be with you. I wish every happiness for you and your family, I know, right now the pain is stronger but...Vashti, from time to time...if you need us we're here, all fans of Andy will forever be with you in spirit. Sincerely,

—*Elizabeth Segarra*
Spain

So hard to believe this time has gone by without him...Not a day goes by that I don't think of him and his family. I pray every day for them, for GOD to give them strength and courage to go on without him, until they can be together again. I wish them nothing but love and I take comfort in knowing that Andy is looking down on them from heaven, missing them as much as they are missing him.
Forever in my heart...

—*Kim Minniti*
USA

TRIBUTE

I was wondering, after having watched *Gabriel* for the millionth time, whether the realm between heaven and hell is us as we are now? Maybe it's our fate that has yet to be decided and it was Andy's fate to walk with the angels because he had a pure soul? I'm not sure, but I do know that he is and always will be loved by everyone whose hearts he touched, even in such a short time. I hope that we are all destined to meet him one day when our fate has been decided...

x x x Missing You Always Andy x x x

—*Jill "Dillymoo" Swindell*
Newcastle, UK

I'm a slave to my feelings, I live with my sadness...You gave it all, without asking, gave me emotions, laughter, the feelings, and continue in the memories...But you left, you left without saying goodbye, and I understand! You did not know of my existence, but without knowing it, you were with me, because you were part of my life. I've never met you personally, but your work came to me, as a fluke, and now I cannot forget! You left your physical body, to be a spiritual body, which cannot be seen or touched, and we are left with empty hands, with the heavy hearts and tired eyes of mourning!! There is no consolation! Now you live in paradise, free from sorrow and pain, and we are happy for you...but our pain is not relieved, because you live in our hearts!

Andy, Thanks for your existence!

—*Lidia E. García*
Gran Canaria, Spain

Andy Whitfield 1971-2011

I saw him when I watched *Spartacus*, and to be honest, at first he didn't impress me. But I liked the show itself, so I watched episode after episode and Andy became more and more important for me with every minute on the screen. Then came the horrible news—He was diagnosed...

Having such bad experiences with this disease I was deeply depressed. And then the great news—he was in remission and was preparing for *Spartacus's* next season. I couldn't wait. Saw his pictures without hair, saw him weakened after the treatment but it was HIM and nothing could make him look bad. Then more horrible news, and then I had my birthday on Sept 11. The worst birthday ever. Nothing has been the same since that day...

—*Monika Jakubowska*
Poland

Vashti,

I just want to let you know that you are always in my thoughts and in my heart...just like Andy...I just hope that every day that passes...I don't want to say gets easier...because it never will, my darling. I don't know sometimes what to say, I just want you to know that I'm here...sweep your darling babies into your arms and give them the biggest cuddle. You are my hero, my special lady...love to you and the babies; keep strong Vashti...just remember we love you...xxxxx

—*Irene*
London

TRIBUTE

It has been several weeks since I felt the world slip slightly off its axis with the passing of Andy Whitfield. There are no words to express my grief and sadness at such an enormous loss to his family, friends, fans and cast mates. I will be forever grateful for the thirteen episodes of *Spartacus Blood and Sand* in which he embodied all of the heart, strength, courage and grace of the character he so brilliantly portrayed. Though I am certain it has been difficult moving forward with the production of *Spartacus* without him, the fans will find a way to continue to embrace this show, the likes of which I have never before seen in my lifetime, and I have no doubt Andy would have wanted it so. He will always be a part of that legacy, and he will never be forgotten by those blessed to know and love him personally, and those of us who loved and admired him from afar.

—*Jodi Moyer Lane*
Colborne, Ontario, Canada

Weeks pass...I don't really know what to say; it seems a long time, but it still hurts like hell. Your life was snatched away from you; you were snatched away from your family...and taken from us...a life cut short. What makes me sad is that we will never see your future work; all we have are memories...we will never see how amazing you would have become...More tears...With love and respect for Vashti Jesse and Indigo...they are always in my thoughts and prayers.
I miss you still so much...xxxxxx

—*Irene*
London

Andy Whitfield 1971-2011

A letter to our angel in heaven...Andy. We are living each day as if it were the last, after you left we realized how valuable it is to be in this world, a lesson that unfortunately we had to learn by your leaving us; you have been claimed in heaven for a mission as important as you had on earth, we know that you care and protect your family from heaven and our messages will be delivered there. We were lucky to meet you even shortly before your departure; that is the most precious gift that God has made us. We are sad but we are proud to have been able to hear from you, learn and to become better people by just looking into your eyes. We are missing you, but we know you'll always be in our hearts and our thoughts.

Thanks Andy, I never get tired of saying thank you for offering us such a valuable gift, your presence. We love you now and always. Be happy beautiful angel.

—*Elizabeth Segarra*
Spain

Vashti,

To write these words, I can't stop crying, because your pain, greater than mine, than of all of us, is ours. It's a pain that destroys all resistance, ability to think, act, and understand WHY. We all suffer the loss of our dear Andy.

Nothing and nobody can bring your love, yours and our dear Andy back; we can only try to give you comfort with our words, our strength, our prayers and our thoughts that are always with you and your children.

God bless and protect you with Andy looking out for you...

—*Lavinia Goretti Carmona*
Lisbon, Portugal

TRIBUTE

A beautiful being, a special being walked to the other side. I'm feeling respect and admiration for you, because first of all you were a man, a father and a husband...many images, many smiles, many feelings, a big heart in this world, an angel to fly high! Months have passed and the road still looks very sad...

We laugh every day, we live, breathe every day, but there is always time for you to come into my mind and make me see your face in my memory. I remember you always!

Prayers for Vashti and the children, and also prayers for all the people who love you; I am one of those people! We miss you...we love you... all of us have a part of you in their heart; we all suffer the loss, and all join our hands to share the pain.

Do not forget us, Andy, because we do not forget you...Thank you.

—Lidia E. García
Gran Canaria, Spain

Dear Vashti,

I'm sure you have wonderful memories of your husband and I'm sure that you'll cherish them forever. I send my heartfelt condolences to you, I know that you and the kids will stay strong and keep his memory alive. Andy will always be in our hearts and thoughts, RIP Andy, a true champion.

—Nancy Decker
Istanbul, Turkey

Andy Whitfield 1971-2011

Even after all these weeks since his passing, I find it very hard to believe that he's gone. How can our Champion of Capua, Bringer of Rain, be gone? I'm completely obsessed with the show and Andy played a huge part in that, he was so perfect as Spartacus. I know that he had to wait a long time for an opportunity like that, but it was worth the wait, he was born to play Spartacus.

I felt a real connection, a special bond as soon as I saw him; he was really unique in that sense. I know that he fought very hard to be rid of the disease, I admire his courage and strength, and he was a true champion, both on screen and in real life.

His passing broke my heart into a million pieces, he was taken from us way too soon. He was supposed to keep playing Spartacus and see his babies grow up. I get sad every time I think about how happy his baby girl Indigo Sky looked in his arms. I still cry every time I remember his last words to them, I can't even imagine how hard saying goodbye to them must have been. It's such a tragedy.

I walk in your shadow every day, I will follow you till the end of time...my heart breaks at your passing...maybe one day we will meet in heaven...that day cannot come too soon...my prayers and thoughts go to your family...they miss you more than I, but never doubt in your mind...we will all be together...in the kingdom of heaven...love you, miss you...xxxxxx

—Irene
England

TRIBUTE

We have a new angel in heaven. I think he's surrounded by love, which was always transmitted in the material world, and I will continue to pray for him and his beautiful family!

—*Giselle Nydia Ferreirós*
Buenos Aires, Argentina

Eternal Love

The sun will be clouded forever
And the sea dried up in an instant.
The axis of the earth will be broken like fragile crystal.
Everything will happen.
Death will cover me with its funereal crepe
But will never extinguish
The flame of my love for you.

—G. A. Becquer

The strength of our love and admiration for you will always keep alive the flame of your memory....forever loved and deeply missed, my dear and precious Andy

—*Inés*
Spain

Love you Andy. RIP, we will never forget you xxx

—*Chi Cetin*
USA

Andy Whitfield 1971-2011

To Vashti...

From this wonderful group headed by Penny Douglas we want to join your family, albeit only in thought and only for one day, this sad day but with so much love in our hearts. Vashti, we light three candles for you and the two children, Jesse and Indigo. "Faith moves mountains, but Andy moves all our dear planet earth". Thank you for staying with him until his last moments. We love you.

—Elizabeth Segarra
Spain

You will always be in our hearts.

—Paola
Italy

Life goes on, and we follow, that is our fate. But it is difficult, we need something, a part of all of us flew to heaven. He lives entangled in our thoughts, he lives around our hearts, and he lives always in our breath. He's the sea that my eyes see...He's the air I breathe every day... He's in my mind in every moment...He lives in me, and is gone from the physical world, but he continues in the spiritual realm, the one we cannot see or touch. You were an important person in my life although I did not personally know you, but...thanks for being part of my life...

He came to this world through the love of his parents. He lived and grew, and managed to reach the arms of a beautiful woman. With his wife he started a family, and had two wonderful children. And their children are the reason he is still here...They will be Andy's footsteps in this, our world!! I can only think of your wife and your children...and pray for them, and I'm still here, they are the reason!

—Lidia E. García
Gran Canaria, Spain

I started watching *Spartacus Blood and Sand* on my birthday in September 2011, completely oblivious to the fact that the magnificent warrior on TV had only a week left to live. It was not before episode four that I went online to find information about the actor who had caught my attention, only to find out that he had passed away just a few days before. I read he had played the role of an angel before that, and found it so symbolic. And there I was, shedding tears about a complete stranger who had touched my heart in a magical way. Andy Whitfield is so genuine and powerful in his role as Spartacus, so strong and so fragile at the same time, so passionate and calm...absolutely genius. He lightened up every scene with his presence. I felt for him, cried with him and laughed with him. One may wonder what other astonishing pieces of work he could have delivered in the long and successful career that he inevitably would have had; sadly he had actually given us the performance of a lifetime, his swan song. It is a tragic and inconceivable loss of a young life, but Andy had just enough time to complete his

Andy Whitfield 1971-2011

inspiring gift to all of us and to spend time with his family and tell them how much he loved them. I am sure he felt the love he inspired flow back to him. He spoke about having fearlessness he had never experienced before, and I know this is how he has faced the battle of his life. And even now, after the light in his eyes has faded away, he manages to connect and touch the hearts of more and more people. God bless his soul and watch over his wife and children.

—Ivanka Ivkova
Leuven, Belgium
(originally from Sofia, Bulgaria)

The world has lost one of the greatest actors to ever grace our screens; we mourn the loss of such talent and the heights he could achieve. But a wife lost her husband and children lost their father. For this we are greatly saddened and pray for comfort in these dark days.

A humble and honorable man, RIP Andy.

—Lori Rose Baard
Australia

TRIBUTE

One day my boyfriend came home from his work trip and said, darling, you know what? My colleagues recorded the series *Spartacus* and I asked: what is that? He replied: when you see it you'll like it...When I saw the first episode I liked everything because I love action, but I had not paid much attention to the actor, until the third chapter. My boyfriend had to resume his travels and one day he came back and said the actor of Spartacus had been diagnosed with cancer. It grieved me because I had loved ones who have suffered from the disease. In the end I finished watching the entire series, and had paid more attention to the actor and went on to search the internet about his history and he captivated me a lot; I like everything about him, so I started looking for Andy fans to follow and support him having high hopes that he could heal, but life is not so. Today he is as a member of my family and I feel like he is a brother, a cousin etc. Strange! I often ask myself why and I reached deep inside my heart to find the answer:

Andy was a humble person, magical in his angelic looks, a great husband, father, brother and son. One doesn't need to travel to discover his life; he is just as he was seen by his audience.

That's how I came to know you and I'm sad because I would have liked to have known you much earlier, but today I find it very difficult to express my feelings when I post a photo of you. I find joy because you were to be you although I mourn and cry out loud because you left; I wish it was not so. I miss you much and I know there will be a time when we'll meet in your new home.

Rest in peace Andy Whitfield.

—*Alejandra Raggiotti*
Buenos Aires, Argentina

Andy Whitfield 1971-2011

The world without you, not the same! A great loss to us, but an incalculable loss to your family. Missing you! You know Andy, when I look one of your photos, one picture with a great smile, you're the sun, and you're the light of my day! You have so much power over me!

You're not here, but when I think about you it makes me smile. You're not here, but your work, your beautiful work, makes me smile, too. You're not here, but I'm thinking so often of your children, a part of you. The thought makes me smile.

I know, you're not here, but you're alive in me. You're a wonderful angel, with beautiful blue wings, a guardian angel for your family! It has been almost two months since your departure to a distant place we cannot see. We cannot touch you. We cannot forget!

I thank you for having existed, and having come into my life. I give thanks from my heart and I invite you to come to my dreams, because the dreams are a real world, too!

You're the power, the light, the love and the eternity!

—*Lidia E. García*
Gran Canaria, Spain

"Falling"...Gabriel..."far from grace"... But NO, not at all...We are ALL completely IN HIS GRACE!

11-11-11 at 11:11 EST: In my meditation I saw ALL OF US... present here on Earth or on the other side...Andy, my dad, my grandmother...others...all of you, Vashti, Jesse, Indigo ...all of my *Spartacus* friends...ALL OF US!

Floating, basking in warm, loving, golden light...HIS GRACE, the divine spirit, the universe...so totally pervasive

TRIBUTE

it fills, caresses, carries ALL OF US!

Do not despair! Lidia, Lavinia, Irene and others...don't be so sad...we ALL are spiritual beings. Right now, some of us are having a physical experience...but we will return to the spiritual realm. Soon... in the blink of an eye if you consider eternity. Let's not forget to make the most out of this physical experience, though.

Let's be kind to each other and to all living things as they, too, carry the divine spark. Let's not worry all the time; it will not change things for the better. Let's not fret and be angry, lest we do more damage than good to ourselves and others. Let's work hard and be humble to make a positive difference in this life. Let's be grateful for our many blessings and continue to do so every day.

May we all feel the love and joy that the divine light brings to ALL OF US. EVERY DAY!

—Irena,
Reiki Master, New York

Vashti...Jesse...and Indi...I think of you often...you're never far away from my thoughts. I'm sending lots of love and prayers to you. I still have a very sad heart as I am sure you have...we lost one hell of a man...he will be missed forever that's for sure...big hugs and lots of love for you all...xxxxxx

—*Irene*
London

Andy Whitfield 1971-2011

Conserva lo que tienes...olvida lo que te duele... lucha por lo que quieres...valora lo que posees... perdona a los que te hieren y disfruta a los que te aman. Nos pasamos la vida esperando que pase algo...y lo único que pasa es la vida. No entendemos el valor de los momentos, hasta que se han convertido en recuerdos. Por eso, haz lo que quieras hacer, antes de que se convierta en lo que te "gustaría" haber hecho. No hagas de tu vida un borrador, tal vez no tengas tiempo de pasarlo en limpio...

Translation:

Retain what you have...forget what hurts...fight for what you want...value what you have...forgive those who hurt you and enjoy those you love. We spend our lives waiting for something to happen...and all that happens is life. We do not understand the value of moments in time, until they have become memories. So do what you like to do before it becomes what you "like" to have done. Do not make your life a rough draft; many times you won't have the opportunity to clean it up...

—*María Del Carmen García*
Córdoba, Spain

A beautiful face, a clean smile, a melodious voice, a man who captured my heart.

Andy, I think of you as an important part of my life, but I can let you go out and rest in peace.

If I let you go out, it makes me suffer, I know...The days pass, the months pass, and you remain in the memories in my mind, forever...Now is the time for you to fly off into the immense universe of stars. You should fly and not suffer for our sorrow and our tears, you have a vested right, the right to be released from this imperfect world, because you are a perfect being in the heavens, and within your spiritual state, are liberated forever.

Right now, you do not suffer in the physical life; this condition makes you a magic man, a man of much lightness with the gift of stroking the face of the people you love without being seen... You are a special being, you are an Angel!! My Angel, our Angel, Andy Whitfield!

Rest in peace, flying freely!!! I miss you so much... Thank you Andy!

—*Lidia E. García*
Gran Canaria, Spain

On a nearby branch
a butterfly alights
breathtakingly beautiful
its wings illuminated by the sun
It hovers tentatively for a moment
and then, resumes its eternal passage
unaware that it has enriched the world
with its beauty.

—*Denise Heid*
USA

Andy Whitfield 1971-2011

On October 17th, 1971, a day a new flower bloomed, with brilliant rainbow colors, and buds like wings of a butterfly. He had eyes that lit up the sky, like the sun that lit up the world. He was born with a heart of gold and a gentle soul. This flower was named Andy Whitfield and on that day an Angel was born, not knowing how his birth would one day change the lives of millions and his life would leave an imprint on the hearts and souls of all who knew him. As this flower grew more beautiful, his name became famous, by portraying an archangel and by playing the historical figure Spartacus, a role that propelled him into the star he was born to be.

Then God decided his time here on earth was done and he needed him back home. He fought, like the warrior he was, for eighteen months, with all he had, with Vashti by his side and with all his family, friends and devoted fans rooting and praying for him.

Then, on September 11th, 2011, the Bringer of Rain left us peacefully, surrounded by love, his butterfly wings broken, as were all our hearts. God took him home, to end his suffering, to end his pain, to give him a crown of jewels and a rope of white and wings to fly upon Heaven's sky. We may never understand why God takes the ones we love, but just know and believe one day we will see Andy again, at Heaven's door, with open arms, greeting us at Heaven's gate, to our new home.

We know he is watching over his loving, supportive wife and his two adoring children Jesse and Indigo, who will grow up knowing what kind of man and loving father he was. I know Vashti is a great mother and will raise them to love, respect and cherish every day of their lives and to never take anything for granted. Andy, you will be immortal, the sound of your name will be endless and you will always have enduring fame.

Not only because of being the loving actor, warrior and

TRIBUTE

champion you were and always will be, but for also being the loving husband, father, son, friend and strong activist and a true hero in life as you will be for all eternity.

Rest in Peace Andy...Gone, but NEVER forgotten.

—*Patti T.*
USA

Friendship, when well cared for, expands as a full blast of color and precious feelings, emitting light and heat. You too, Andy, with your eyes and your smile, you transmit your light and your love to all of us and will forever...

—Lavinia Goretti Carmona
Lisbon, Portugal

Hi Andy,

It's been weeks...this doesn't get any easier...it's my daughter's thirtieth birthday today...I should be happy...but all I can think about is you...it's still so painful I really struggle some days I can't stop thinking about your family, about Vashti, Jesse and Indigo...wondering how they're coping. Your beautiful strong wife and your amazing children; we are all still very very sad...miss you like crazy...you were so much loved Andy, you still are...you will always be loved...and never forgotten...two months later we're still grieving...my love and prayers for your family and the most heartfelt love for you as always...I love you Andy, that's forever...xxxxxxx

—*Irene*
London

Andy Whitfield 1971-2011

Two months have passed and we still cry for you and ask why. Why did you leave? You deserve to be happy, very happy. A man like you deserved it. Your eyes say so much and now we cannot look into your beautiful blue eyes, tender, quiet, to see what is going on inside you. Yes, it was easy to understand. Your eyes were talking for you. We are without our prince, we lost someone wonderful.

The world is without your ray of light. How we miss you, Andy! What pain and anger! It is very unfair. It should not have happened to you, Andy I miss you...always.

—Lavinia Goretti Carmona
Lisbon, Portugal

My little star
shining and gentle
you're so high in the sky, blue-eyed...
The sky is so endless and this is no coincidence
but remember: one star among the countless stars
will always be just you -
My one star! With none will it be replaced.
This is for you Andy.
My star.

—Eleanora Boianova
Vidin, Bulgaria

TRIBUTE

Broken Chain

We little knew that morning
that God was going to call your name.
In life we loved you dearly,
in death we do the same.
It broke our hearts to lose you,
you did not go alone;
for part of us went with you
the day God called you home.
You left us peaceful memories,
your love is still our guide,
and though we cannot see you,
you are always by our side.
Our family chain is broken
and nothing seems the same,
but as God calls us one by one,
the chain will link again.

—Ron Tranmer

—*Audrey Gorman*
Pompano Beach, Florida,

It's your name day...my personal angel Andy...and I'm
with you...more than yesterday and less than tomorrow.

—*Marina*
Italy

Andy Whitfield 1971-2011

You are the breeze that passes and touches my face. You are the star up high that shines brighter in the darkness of the night. You are the absence that saddens days and the pain that lacerates the soul...

Where are you? Your body no longer exists and now where are you? I try to soothe this extreme pain...that I feel since you are gone...

This pain that is lodged inside of my soul... I miss you Andy.

—Lavinia Goretti Carmona
Lisbon, Portugal

After *Blood and Sand*, God took your hand and said your time has come. The gap in our heart is always there. It reminds us that life isn't fair. It's a scar that will never leave our souls, and because of it we feel we will never be whole. With every butterfly we see, we think of you. Time does heal all wounds. However, wounds fade into scars, becoming less visible, but the scar remains as a reminder of the pain. These scars don't make us weak, they mean we still miss you, we remember you, and we wish you were still here. We will gladly cry forever to never forget. Sometimes we feel like it is impossible to stop the pain and tears but God makes the impossible, possible.

You are missed here on earth, Andy, and we will never forget you. The memories you left we will cherish forever. When the world weighs heavy on our shoulders, we count on our Angels to help carry it and one of those angels will be our beloved Andy.

—Patti T.
USA

TRIBUTE

The leaves they fall
upon the day that makes a memory
Those pleading eyes,
echoing, silently in me
The final nights
I guard his sleep, I can do without
the fears down deep
There's nothing good in this mourning...
Oh, and I know...
Invested feelings in the one I would outlast
My little friend is getting tired, fading fast...
Did not want to see the signs
Of the dimming flame

Andy Whitfield 1971-2011

I need to have more time
No, I don't want to let you go
Tonight I fear I'll say goodbye to my little friend
Don't want to let you go...
The warmest heart I've found
I lower into the ground
My tears, forever without you
resting under your tree
You have always liked this place
It now belongs to you...
I need to set you free
and go on alone
One day in my feeble timeline
You gave me your heart and stole mine
Tomorrows came too fast for me
to hear your slow, silent goodbye...
The kindest heart I've found
I lowered into the ground
Your smile kept me alive
back when the skies were still
You always liked this place
Now sleep under the tree
I planted here the day
when you were born
I should've been ready,
seen the nearing end
My little old friend, my child.
That day I had to say goodbye
and turn the bend
but I will never let you go

—*Elizabeth Segarra*
Spain

TRIBUTE

Andy had an amazing ability as an actor to take the audience with him in his roles and especially as Spartacus. He made you feel everything he felt (his love, his pain). I did not know you Andy Whitfield, but I feel as though I did. The impression that you have made on me and many people all around the world will never be forgotten. Andy, a gentle soul—loved and missed always. God's Blessings

—*Gail Gilbert*
Sydney, Australia

I tremble when I think of you. You gave me your all, I did not have to ask. You left without saying goodbye, never knew of my existence, but from my place, I prayed so hard for you! I wasn't able to know you personally, but you reached deep into my heart. I'm asking myself what your power was to control my feelings however you wished. You made me feel beautiful emotions with your brilliant work, with your beautiful performance, but I cry with sadness for your absence. Your loss is not easy. I'm trying to learn to live without you, but it's so so hard.

Words cannot convey the reality of my feelings...the reality of sadness and grief...the pain is still here! I am devastated...Not a day passes that I don't think of you...there isn't a single day that I don't pray for you...there was not a single day in my life, since I knew of your illness, that I didn't work spiritually for you...with my angels, my prayers and my thoughts of health and love, and for you! I got up every day hoping to hear about you! I despaired when time passed without news...but I swear, from the bottom of my heart, today I would rather have the same uncertainty, it would be the reason to believe that you would still be alive in this world.

Your photos are there, your videos are there, your great work is also, but YOU are gone, never to return. You left your physical body to move to a spiritual state, we cannot see or touch...I miss you so much! Here, from my place in the wonderful Playa de Las Canteras de Gran Canaria, I write to you, and you know well that my words are full of love and coming from the bottom of my heart...and you know I wish you were here.

Now I can only remember you every day until the end of my days. Right now life goes on, so I have an obligation to follow and to breathe, but I assure you it is very hard; my love and respect for you are very deep... Thank you for having existed...thank you Andy!

—Lidia E. García
Gran Canaria, Spain

I want to tell all my friends and fans of Andy, that this afternoon when I was sleeping I was fortunate to dream of him, I don't know why. He found himself at a beach close to the sea and was so happy, and his face conveyed peace. I wanted to see him closer, and with his eyes he smiled so sweetly at me! And he went towards the sun, I woke up so happy and my heart found some peace.

This was beautiful, I'll never forget it!

—Alejandra Raggiotti
Argentina

TRIBUTE

Veo tu rostro cuando voy caminando, cuando miro al cielo y cuando alguien me sonríe. Tu sonrisa se pinta en el universo mientras su palpitar canta la canción de tu risa. El cielo dibuja tu mirada con las nubes blanquecinas que se deslizan en el viento. Y tu voz suena en mi mente mientras intento recordar que ya te has ido.

Translation:

I see your face when I go out for a walk, when I look up at the sky and when someone gives me a smile. Your smile paints itself on the universe while its beat sings the song of your laugh. The sky draws your look with the whitish clouds that roll on the wind and your voice sounds in my mind while I try to remind myself that you are already gone.

—*Luisa Ramos W.*
Medellin, Colombia

It was a sad day for all of us...the day you were gone forever and left us without your light, your smile, your voice, your wonderful work.

Your presence was necessary for us all. Now, without you, life is different, there is an empty space that no one will fill. I have no words to explain this suffering. Why? I do not know.

I will pray for you and for your children and family. Andy, you are always present in our thoughts. I miss you in all the moments of my life.

—*Lavinia Goretti Carmona*
Lisbon, Portugal

Andy Whitfield 1971-2011

Not a day goes by that I don't think of you, Andy, just seeing a butterfly, or a picture, or seeing a picture of your beautiful wife Vashti or seeing or reading about the two remarkable, amazing, so intelligent for their ages, works of beautiful art that you and Vashti created, Jesse and Indi.

I miss you today, I will miss you tomorrow, I will miss you until the end of time. My sorrow is deep, but even with the grief I still hold from the loss of you, Vashti gives me the motivation to live life to the fullest, because she has shown that true love does exist and that when you lose your soul-mate, your life can't stop, you must carry on and live life and along the way, share the memories of the love you both shared and I'm trying to do just that.

God bless you our loving Champion—Gone, but never forgotten. You have captured the hearts of thousands and even after your death, you captured even more. Your memory will live on through your beautiful children, your amazing wife Vashti, your family, friends and especially, through your fans—we will be here for you always.

Rest in Peace, our Angel

—Patti T.
USA

Something in my mind makes me dream of your sweet and hot eyes that made me feel... and one thousand universes build... maybe in another horizon, your gaze lights me again but for now...I can just, in sorrow...wait.

—Inés
Spain

TRIBUTE

If love could have saved you,
you would have lived forever.
    —Patricia Grant

—*Lottisse Mendoza*
Jacksonville, Florida, USA

I feel your presence in the sunshine
that warms me and lights my path
I feel your presence in the stars
that enchant my night
I feel your presence in the Moon
I feel your presence in the absence
I miss your presence
Missing you we all feel
And that makes us cry all the time
How much I miss you Andy...

—*Lavinia Goretti Carmona*
Lisbon, Portugal

Andy, you are in the arms of God, what a place to be. My prayers are with your family, bless them.

—*Margaret Coville*
Ontario, Canada

Andy Whitfield 1971-2011

When Andy died, my biggest question was why I had been able to recover and heal but he had not. But then, seeing the pointlessness of such a question, I realized I'm here and I have a second chance. I owe it to Andy, and even to my friend, who also died of cancer a few years ago, to really live. To be the best, healthiest, happiest person I can be. Not to mention to follow my dream.

But now I'm almost seeing through Andy's eyes the wondrous world of creativity and talent around me. And I know Andy was a great appreciator of talented people. As a member of the Screen Actors Guild, I am being invited to many screenings now that it is awards season. I've tried to make as many as I am able. And I'm just appreciating all the wonderful work, the creativity involved and all the talented people in these projects.

And it makes me realize there are so many outstanding, talented people out there. Some who may not even have had a chance to shine yet, and it makes me smile because the world is not such a dark place. The world is full of light, if only you look for it.

Andy was one of those lights that shone very brightly, albeit all too briefly. But he has helped me see with new eyes, with a renewed appreciation, and it makes me so happy. It makes me want to be part of it. It makes me want to be the best actress I could possibly be so that one day I, too, will get my moment to shine.

So I want to thank you all for all your comments both positive and negative because it all helped to open my eyes. I'm so grateful to you all for helping me realize that there is so much beauty in the world. So much wonder.

—*Kate Pak*
Teaneck, New Jersey, USA

TRIBUTE

A man is reborn without limitation…lives in a spiritual state, not earthly…but his light is still here. Now the man is immortal, has been reborn and resurrected, he's a man free and vastly lighter, embraced in a life of joy and without suffering and sorrow. That's you, Angel Andy! The beauty in the heavens.

—Lidia E. García
Gran Canaria, Spain

I know for certain that we never lose the people we love, not even to death. They continue to participate in every act, thought and decision we make. Their love leaves an indelible imprint in our memories. We find comfort in knowing that our lives have been enriched by having shared their love.

—Karen Pressley
Sheffield, UK

I have not been here on Facebook for a while, Andy, but I still think of you every day, miss you immensely, and love you so much. Keep shining bright; the brightest star in the sky, our Gladiator, our Champion, our Andy xxxx

—Jeannette Smith
England

Andy Whitfield 1971-2011

Every day...every hour...every minute...always and forever...Andy you are in my heart and in my mind...

—*Marina*
Italy

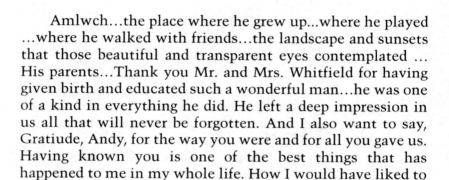

Amlwch...the place where he grew up...where he played ...where he walked with friends...the landscape and sunsets that those beautiful and transparent eyes contemplated ... His parents...Thank you Mr. and Mrs. Whitfield for having given birth and educated such a wonderful man...he was one of a kind in everything he did. He left a deep impression in us all that will never be forgotten. And I also want to say, Gratiude, Andy, for the way you were and for all you gave us. Having known you is one of the best things that has happened to me in my whole life. How I would have liked to thank you personally, shaking your hand, even if it had been just a for a second...

—*Inés*
Spain

Today I thought of Andy. I realize how precious life is and I'm thankful for all my blessings.
RIP Andy, sending lots of prayers for your family.

—*Jessica Zayakosky*
Bel Air, Maryland, USA

TRIBUTE

Andy...life goes on, I smile, breathe and live every day, but every day I do remember you...at any time of the day, you get to my thoughts...and you're here with me always. Many weeks passed since your departure, and every 11th of each month, I light a candle for you in my house... And while I can do it, I will do it for you! I need you here, but I know that you cannot come back down here.

Spartacus is not the same without you, because you are essentially Spartacus...you're the show...you're the art! Forever!

—*Lidia E. García*
Gran Canaria, Spain

No more steel in my hands waits in the arena! Speechless and restless...awaiting my terms of survival! Then the gates open, and with that my fears might be answered...but...Spartacus came out no longer, which made me sad! So the steel falls from my hands...and I face the sky. "This wasn't a fair fight," I screamed! "You could have given this a true fight, but why take away our Spartacus?" Only silence is left. A final thrill went through the air...images of the mighty Andy—Spartacus—rushed through the arena. Oh, boy! When the dust settled...and the sky cleared...I knew we had lost one of the biggest warriors of all time! We miss you Andy!

—*Perry TheCrow*
USA

Andy Whitfield 1971-2011

Eleven long long weeks, Vashti my darling, all we can do is send our love and prayers to you all. I think of you and Jesse and Indigo every day...I'm still very very sad...but I'm wishing you with all my heartfelt love: keep strong, missy, and big big hugs for you Jesse, Indigo and of course for Andy our champion...he is so missed still...love...

—*Irene*
London

Andy, I searched in the moonlight the image of your face, in the stars the brightness of your eyes that enchanted us. But all I found was missing you. Longing that doesn't pass with time. The tears running down my face do not hurt. What hurts is the reason that they do fall, it is your absence, they fall for you leaving us.

—*Lavinia Goretti Carmona*
Lisbon, Portugal

Today you've been in my thoughts...I remember the words you said to your children...I returned today to mourn for you...The love for you is present always, because you're a special person! I need you...I miss you!

—*Lidia E. García*
Gran Canaria, Spain

TRIBUTE

Vashti, Jesse and Indigo,

I don't think that I can ever explain in words my first reaction when I saw Andy play the role of Spartacus. From the very first episode I was hooked. His ability to show compassion, love and sorrow in his acting really truly affected me. Looking into his eyes, you felt like you were looking into his soul, and though we never met, I am sure that had to have come from a place within him. Andy was not only a champion in *Spartacus*, but in life as well.

I have met nine wonderful women whom I have become great friends with from around the world. We have all become an inspiration to each other and we will always continue to be great friends. That never would have happened without Andy. He has affected all of our lives in so many ways.

My heart goes out to you and your children. You will always be in my thoughts and prayers and know that he will be missed but never forgotten.

—Lisa Swanson
Michigan, USA

Your life was so beautiful, like butterflies in the summer days, with colors as bright as a rainbow. Then your life was taken, your wings broke and so did our hearts and that's why we are crying...You left us with memories that will last forever. First you were a Warrior, then you became a slave; once in the arena, a Champion was made. Now that you are gone, you are an Angel, with soaring wings, as white as the whitest cloud, watching over Vashti, Jesse and Indigo. With each butterfly they see, they will know it is you. You will be missed forever, and the memories you gave us will last a lifetime.

Rest in Peace, our loving Angel...Andy

—Patti T.
USA

Andy's life had more purpose than we will ever realize. I, too, never met this wonderful, passionate, graceful, and loving man, but he left a mark in this world. I have always heard God takes the "good ones." Just look what has happened in our world because of the life of one man and the mark he left. God gave us his Son to forgive us our sins so that we may live...I believe Andy's life was a testimony to what he believed and to the type of person we could be.

Ever since this Facebook page was started by our beloved Penny, there have been many friendships made, people have come together in prayer for our loved ones including Andy, Danny, Mare, myself, Penny, and many more. These are the things that stand as a true testament of time and friendship. Is this not what Andy showed in his brief life here on earth?

I believe he is in heaven with the holy of all God. I truly feel this thing we have here is a wonderful connection called love...that was demonstrated to us by Andy in all that he did, even in death. God would be pleased with the effect that Andy had on all of us...I just don't want us to lose sight of the fact that Andy was a follower of a greater kind and we should take from his life the lessons that he, too, followed. Those were the things that made us all love him so much.

—Kendra J Newman
Yauhannah, South Carolina, USA

TRIBUTE

Dear Andy,

Thank you, thank you for your extraordinary work, for all your dedication and commitment, for all the effort to continue chasing a dream, for choosing to be an actor and doing so well. Thank you for sacrificing time with your family; thanks to Vasthi for that too. Your fight for life is an inspiration to all of us.

We carry in our hearts your blues eyes; clean and serene. Death took away the man, but did not remove the legend... You will be in our souls for all eternity.

With all my love to Vasthi and the children,

—Blanca
Spain

Everyone who ever met him said he was a genuinely nice man. Why do we always lose the nice ones?

> *A heart of gold stopped beating,*
> *two shining eyes at rest,*
> *God broke our hearts to show us*
> *he only takes the best...*
> —Author Unknown

—Clancy Ellis
London, UK

Andy Whitfield 1971-2011

No one knows the silent heartache
Only those who have loved can tell
The grief we bear in silence
For the one we loved so well.
The tears in our eyes we wipe away
but the pain in our hearts is here to stay
The dearest friend the Earth could hold
The kindest smile and heart of gold.
To all who knew you, all will know
Just what we lost awhile ago.
We mourn but dare not question why
God called him home just when
His future seemed secure and bright
We only pray to meet again.
　　　　　　　　　—Author Unknown

Good night, Andy, we love you.

　　　　　　　　　　　—Anna Pacilio
　　　　　　　　　　New Jersey, USA

Dear Andy,

Months have passed and I can't forget you... You have left a mark so deep in my heart that I can feel your soul in all I do. I know you are looking after your loving wife and your beautiful children, but perhaps they can't imagine how you have changed the life of a lot of people who knew you in one or another way, connected with you, and after this, I think, we are better persons. Only because we have seen how you fought to become what you wanted to be, and the way you did it, with respect, with hard work, helping other people, being yourself, feet on the ground all time...and, unfortunately, we also have seen how fate is so wrong sometimes, so unfair. And we either don't understand or we don't want to understand; we refuse the truth, refuse to believe that you have gone, you have left...How I wish I were able to do that...Things would be easier for all of us... Lots of kisses and hugs from Spain.

—*E.F.*
Spain

A few weeks, seems like an eternity. I remember you and miss you so much. You live in me, in my heart, in my mind, in my thoughts. The grief and sorrow are still here, but we must continue. I remember you every day, you come to my thoughts. I pray for myself, because all of us have lost. You're not here. So sad, so hard...I miss you because you are a part of me! You're the eternity. You're the beauty!
Andy Whitfield, our Angel in heaven!

—*Lidia E. García*
Gran Canaria, Spain

Andy Whitfield 1971-2011

The magnitude of a person cannot be measured by the space that he or she occupies in our hearts, but by the emptiness that is left when he or she leaves. And the emptiness that you left has no end, Andy...

You are always in our hearts.

—*Lavinia Goretti Carmona*
Lisbon, Portugal

Dear Andy,

You touched so many hearts, especially mine, at a time when I knew nothing of your struggle with cancer and my son had just been diagnosed with this terrible disease. My heart was broken and I knew not whether he was going to be with us for Christmas.

During his treatment, I escaped with *Spartacus* and with you. You were the most handsome man I had ever, ever seen. Your role as Spartacus touched my heart, I wanted to be the woman you loved, I wanted to have you survive against all odds for the love you had for me. I needed escape.

I then found out of your illness, and all the while heard that you were doing well, that you were getting better and that everyone was happy with your progress. This gave me inspiration and hope as my son, also a brave fighter, was coping with his treatment well. Then, following my son's final chemotherapy cycle, he took a turn for the worse and was straight back in hospital on a drip, lifeless and broken. That is when your life had slipped from your broken body.

Oh, Andy, how I cried and cried. I felt so desperate and sad, that somehow you and my son had been through so much together. I was in shock. My son has beat cancer (for now) and the pain I felt for you has subsided, but I feel the pain of your dearest wife and babies, that you are no longer with them. Oh, how I wish that I could meet Vashti to hug her and tell her that she is not alone.

Rest in peace my sweet Andy, you were so much and so many things to so many of us, and to Vashti, you were her man who loved her and whom she has fought for. She is a lucky lady.

God rest your soul. XXXXX
Forever a warrior, love from

—Diana and her Maximo
Bunbury, Cheshire, UK

He was such a gentle, humble guy. There was something so serene about him. He wasn't what I was expecting Spartacus to be. He brought something quite unique to the role. Thank you, Andy.

—Mary D.
Sydney, Australia

Such a beautiful, talented young man that was taken away too soon! He communicated with his fans, which was nice of him to do. I prayed for him, but the Lord needed him in his garden of angels. He is no longer in pain. He will never be forgotten. I'm sure his wife sees him in his children's eyes. He is now watching over his children and wife. I would've liked to have seen his acting career go farther, but I'm glad to have been able to enjoy him as Spartacus. He was a wonderful young man and he will not be forgotten! Love...

—Your fan from
Huntsville, Alabama, USA

Andy Whitfield 1971-2011

HE...The earth, our planet Earth, the cosmos would disappear deleting all without...him. He...so important, more than the air that helps us to live, as the sun that warms our Earth, as the moon, bright in her magnificence when we're looking at the full moon, as the brilliant stars bringing us a dream in the night... This is he...necessary, essential...

—*Elizabeth Segarra*
Spain

Andy,

Some people come into our lives
and leave footprints on our hearts
and we are never ever the same.
Some people come into our lives
and quickly go...Some stay for awhile
and embrace our silent dreams.
They help us become aware
of the delicate winds of hope...
and we discover within every human spirit
there are wings yearning to fly.
—Flavia Weedn

How I wish I could have met you, to let you know what you mean to me... An extraordinarily wonderful man of character. So gentle and kind, who touched our lives briefly, but won over our hearts forever.

I will always remember your smile and keep it close to my heart always...until I'm called home to heaven

Love

—*Kim*
USA

TRIBUTE

The Sun and the Moon are still here. The world keeps turning, it is the law of life. You're gone forever; we're lost knowing we cannot see your face again, your beautiful blue eyes and your sweet and pretty smile. The world is so different. All the love we lost—a piece of our heart! Your pictures are not enough...

—*Lidia E. García*
Gran Canaria, Spain

Andy Whitfield 1971-2011

Andy, a true man who got into my life, a true man who devoted body and soul to his family for, sadly, only a very short time. Andy, a true man who came into my life and conquered my heart without trying, a true man who makes me meet people who share the sadness of his departure and his loss, a true man who went away never to come back. Now we have to learn to live without you, we all cry for you, we all miss you, because you got deep into our hearts, because you were, you are and you will be a special being forever, for eternity!

I love you.

—Pilar
The Canary Islands, Spain

How could I be so captivated by someone I never met? Andy was truly unique and reached into our hearts and souls. He is one of a kind, a truly amazing person. Thank you Mr. and Mrs. Whitfield for raising such a wonderful human being who was a wonderful son, brother, husband, father, and friend. He was embraced by so many who never had the pleasure of meeting him personally. He was a gift to us all!

I have become the greatest of friends with many because of the mutual love and admiration we have for Andy. We all hope to be able to one day meet in person. A dream come true! Vashti, "Thank you" for sharing Andy with us through his career. Vashti, Jesse and Indigo Sky you will always be in the hearts and prayers of the fans from all over the world. Sincerely and much Love...

—Bonnie Lynn Armendariz
Hawaii, USA

TRIBUTE

Eight Months without our Angel

Anoche pude sentirte en mis sueños
Pude perderme en tu mirada y ahogarme
en su azul profundo
Pude deleitarme con tu risa
Y danzar con la melodía dulce del sonido de tu voz.
Pude ver esa belleza que se ha extinguido de la tierra
Ese fuego que pareció apagarse hace ya 8 meses
Y aun así, pude disfrutar de esa sublimidad
Y calentarme con tu fuego azul y con tu silencio
o tu voz
Aun así tuve que despertar
Y la desazón me lleno mientras la amargura
se posaba en mis labios
Dejando ese sabor a tristeza y a mañana nublada,
Pero entonces supe que no querrías tal cosa
Me dibujé una sonrisa y enfrente el día con tu aroma,
Tu fuego, tu mirada y tu sonrisa
marcados en el interior de mis parpados

Translation:

Last night I could feel you in my dreams
I could get lost in your gaze
and be drowned in its deep blue
I could take delight with your laughter
And could dance to the sweet melody
of the sound of your voice.
I could see that beauty now extinguished from this earth
That fire that seemed to have gone out of this world
already eight months ago
And still, I could enjoy that sublimity
And get warmed with your blue fire
and your silence or your voice

Andy Whitfield 1971-2011

Still I had to be awakened
And the uneasiness took over
while the bitterness placed itself on my lips
Leaving this taste of sadness and clouded morning
But then I knew you wouldn't want such a thing
I drew on my face a smile
and faced the day with your scent,
your fire, your look and your smile
tattooed on the back of my eyelids

—*Luisa Ramos W.*
Medellin, Colombia

Sorry to have lost you, but glad to have known you, dear Andy. You were a great man, who had captured so many hearts in such a way that only few actors ever had. There was the truth in your eyes, which, seen only once, could never be forgotten. In my eyes you were true perfection as a man, as a person, as a fighter. With you, the world was a better place...

—*Ekaterina Mikriukova*
Moscow, Russia

Oh, you fought to the end of your devastating battle. Our hearts ache that you are no longer here with us today. Every day I look outside and see the butterflies fly beneath the clouds, I believe it's the path to heaven. We miss you Andy. Life's a journey. Life's a battle. Nobody ever said life

TRIBUTE

was going to be easy. Andy, you don't know how much we wish you were here with us today. We all don't really know much about you, but we have heard and seen enough—the loving man, and gentle soul you were. You were a brave man you fought to the end...Just like a true Champion
RIP Brother

—*Patti T.*
USA

Don't grieve for me, for now I'm free,
I'm following the path God has laid you see.
I took his hand when I heard his call.
I turned my back and left it all.
I could not stay another day
To laugh, to love, to work or play.
Tasks left undone must stay that way
I found the peace at the close of day.
If my parting has left a void
Then fill it with remembered joys-
A friendship shared, a laugh, a kiss
Oh yes, these things I too will miss.
Be not burdened with times of sorrow
I wish you the sunshine of tomorrow.
My life's been full I savored much,
Good friends, good times, a loved one's touch.
Perhaps my time seemed all too brief
Don't lengthen it now with undue grief
Lift up your hearts, and peace to thee-
God wanted me now, he set me free.
—Linda Jo Jackson

—*Poem selected by Bonnie Lynn Armendariz*
Hawaii, USA

Andy Whitfield 1971-2011

Warrior Angel

A glimpse of Glory
Abrupt and cruel
Of Warrior Angel
And Playful Fool
Of a Husband's love
And a Father's Devotion
Skilled Actor rendering
Powerful emotion
 Of Dearest Friend
And Loyalty most deep
Memories of laughter
And that triumphant leap
Of an easy ready Grin
And body lean and long
And piercing blue Eyes
Face angular and strong
A flicker of light
Windswept then extinguished
Of Not Yet Appreciated
Then Suddenly Distinguished
Some Warmth yet remains
As Fighting Soul departs
From Love still fresh
In loved ones' hearts
Brief Gift of Life
Is received gratefully
This pain is great
But so is his Legacy
Continued Reminiscence
Smile paired with a tear
The Remembered never leave,
Thus Andy is Here.

—*Mirriam Shah*
Springfield, Virginia, USA

TRIBUTE

Immortal

Érase una vez un joven y hermoso guerrero
Era él quien luchaba con ese monstruo
que a tantos mata

Luchaba lento y silencioso
Luchaba sonriendo cada día, cada hora
Con una espada en la mano cual gladiador
Se disponía a recibir las embestidas
De aquel monstruo que desde adentro lo destruía
Ese guerrero tenía el cristal en los ojos
Un cristal tan transparentes
que reflejaba la pureza del cielo
Y la inmensidad del mar
Tenía fuego en la sonrisa,
Un fuego que podía calentar a kilómetros de distancia
Un fuego que podía encender una vida
sin siquiera pronunciar una palabra
No se como me uní al alma de este guerrero
No se como me fundí con el en silencio...
no lo comprendo
Pero una cálida mañana de septiembre
Un soleado domingo de primavera
Ese guerrero dejo caer su espada...
Estaba cansado, estaba herido
Y ya era hora de que iniciara su viaje
a un nuevo mundo

Mi alma unida a la suya,
sintió morir y entonces supe que él por fin
Había ganado esa guerra
Hay quienes dicen que el monstruo
aquel tomo las riendas
y se llevo al guerrero
Pero yo se...
Se lo que paso...

Andy Whitfield 1971-2011

El guerrero depuso sus armas,
dio su cuerpo para ganarle a la vida
El guerrero, engaño al monstruo
                              disfrazándose de muerte
Si buscas a ese monstruo que lo seguía...
no lo podrás encontrar
Pero si buscas al joven y hermoso guerrero,
lo veras en cualquier lugar
Ya que el ahora es inmortal...
siempre joven...siempre hermoso...siempre guerrero

Translation:

Immortal

There once was a handsome young warrior
Who fought against the monster that kills too many
He'd fight slow and silent
He'd fight smiling every day, every hour
With a sword in his hand like a gladiator
He would fight the onslaught
Of the monster that was destroying him from the inside
The warrior had crystal in his eyes
A crystal so clear it reflected the purity of heaven
And the immensity of the sea
He had a fire in his smile
A fire that could light you up from miles away
A fire that could ignite a life without even saying a word
I do not know how I joined my soul with that warrior's
I do not know how I melted with him in silence...
I do not understand
But on a warm September morning
A sunny spring Sunday
This warrior dropped his sword...
He was tired, he was wounded

TRIBUTE

And it was time for him
to begin his journey to a new world
My soul, joined with his, felt dying
And I knew that he finally had won the war
Some say that the monster took the reins
And took the warrior
But I know...I know what happened...
The warrior laid down his arms,
                    gave his body to gain life
The warrior deceived the monster,
disguising himself with death
If you ever try to find the monster
that was chasing him...you will not find it
But if you look for the handsome young warrior,
you will see him everywhere
'Cause he is now immortal...
Always young...Always beautiful...Always a warrior.

—Luisa Ramos W.
Medellin, Colombia

If I could
I would touch the stars,
I would spread flowers in the sky
and would make it rain petals of love,
health and peace ...
just to see your smile again
just to hear your voice again,
dear Andy...miss you so much.

—Lavinia Goretti Carmona
Lisbon, Portugal

Andy Whitfield 1971-2011

A Tribute to Andy Whitfield
For Vashti, Jesse, Indigo and the Whitfield Family,

Your life and your children's lives have just taken a turn down a road none of you asked for. Your lives as you recall them were quite perfect as they were. Your sadness is so overwhelming that it is felt around the world. So much so that a book of Tribute has been produced in Andy's honor.

May this book help you and your children through the years find peace, warm memories and wonderful thoughts of the man you loved as a husband, a father, brother and a son. Andy was an actor who brought life to the character Spartacus that was strong and heroic, a true warrior. Yet, his character showed warmth, honor, passion, integrity and bravery. Much like his very own personality off screen. I had never seen the role of Spartacus played before with such intensity and focus. Andy had the audience from the start and he took them with him to the end. We felt his losses, his pain, emotional and physical, and his triumphs.

It was his skill that compelled us, each week, to watch him on TV and it was his beauty, his unwavering good looks that kept us captivated by him.

Andy was a man to be proud of, a man most of us aspire to be more like. His boyish humor and charm were so infectious they delighted us to no end.

Andy, you are forever with us, for there is no way to forget a man who has given so much of himself to so many. May you feel the love from your family, and your extended family that stretches around the world, for all eternity.

Thank you for leaving us with such a warm impression of the man we've come to love, a man that answered to the name never to be forgotten, "ANDY WHITFIELD".

In loving memory,

—Barbara-Ann Horne
Voice Over Artist, UK

TRIBUTE

With closed eyes, I see you among the flowers,
High above the clouds.
Your presence blows through me with the breeze.
Your smile beams down on through the sun.
The full moon brings the light of your laughter
                                    to my mind.
And the Butterfly in all its splendor reminds me
Of your beauty and freedom now.
Leaving your love for those lingering in this world.

—*Vicki Farine*
Siloam Springs, Arkansas, USA

It has been months...still so sad, still can't believe
you're gone...this is really hard for me to write what I need
to say...it's all been said before...you are and always will be
the young man we grew to love...for your talent for your
human kindness...just because you were you Andy. Funny
beautiful handsome...to me you're not gone...you're still
around. I keep in my heart Vashti, Jesse and Indigo. They are
in my prayers and thoughts. I think of them often.

You're that big shiny star in the sky that I say hi to,blow
a kiss, say goodnight to.

Love and miss you Andy, and that's forever, beautiful
man xxxxxxx

—*Irene*
London, England

Andy Whitfield 1971-2011

It's been months but seems like only yesterday, the sadness has not diminished in the slightest, in fact I think it gets worse day by day! A beautiful family torn apart, our "Andy family" comforting one another as best we can, trying to smile through the tears, I am just glad that Andy lives on in his beautiful children. He will never be forgotten, he lives on in our hearts, our very souls, a man we never got to meet, but he touched us so deeply, we claimed him as our own!

We love and miss you, Andy, and it will never, ever change xxxx

—*Jeannette Smith*
Liverpool, UK

God's Garden

God looked around His garden
And He found an empty place.
And then He looked down
upon the earth,
And saw your tired face.
He put His arms around you,
And lifted you to rest.
God's garden must be beautiful,
He always takes the best.
He knew that you were suffering,
He knew you were in pain,
He knew that you would never
Get well on earth again.
He saw the road was getting rough,

TRIBUTE

And the hills were hard to climb,
So He closed your wary eyelids,
And whispered "Peace be Thine."
It broke our hearts to lose you.
But you didn't go alone,
For part of us went with you,
The day God called you home...
—Mary E. Deforge

You were a loving husband, father, brother, son and friend. There will always be an empty space in our hearts. You will always be in my thoughts and prayers.
God Bless You.

—*Audrey Gorman*
Pompano Beach, Florida, USA

The great pains are silent.
Knowledge exists in the silence that is so profound...
that sometimes it becomes the most perfect answer.
Something exists that is bigger and more pure
than what we say...
Silence takes us from ourselves
Makes us navigate the firmament of spirit,
Brings us closer to heaven.
We sense that the body is nothing more than a prison
In this world that is a place of exile.

—*Lavinia Goretti Carmona*
Lisbon, Portugal

Andy Whitfield 1971-2011

Vashti, good memories are yours... Andy is the sun that warms your face, Andy is the breeze that caresses your face, your precious children are Andy, because your husband is alive in them! You know that feeling will never will go, the love for him is forever...

Hugs and Much love

—Lidia E. García
Gran Canaria, Spain

Sydney, Sunday morning, a sunny day in September... A woman holds a man in her arms...Tears run down her beautiful face. A man, her husband, just passed away. By the looks of it, he fought a battle he could not win. But on his face a serene smile of peace. Free. He's free now. Free of pain and sorrow, free of his earthly body that failed to do what his spirit commanded. His smile—Andy's smile—a smile that moved so many hearts. Forever young, forever in our minds. An Angel now, looking down on us, helping us, always motivating us to live!

To live and love, for love has no boundaries, love goes way beyond that. A man and his legacy: humble, serene, a fighter, a father, a lover, a husband. Forever in our minds, forever in our hearts, forever young...

—Sylke, Brasschaat
Belgium

TRIBUTE

Whilst flicking through the channels on a typical, boring Tuesday night, I stumbled across *Spartacus*. I was instantly fascinated with the show and after watching the first episode I was hooked! I couldn't wait for the next installment and I remember thinking about the show the following day. So much so that I took to Google and Facebook! I typed in "Spartacus" and "Andy Whitfield" and came across his fan page, and information on the actor who portrayed him!

At that time there was only a handful of people and I got to know those people very well. Soon the numbers swelled and I found myself enveloped in a whole new interesting and exciting family! I have so many genuine friends that I care for deeply and speak with every day, all thanks to Andy and the show.

This may all seem trivial, but after two redundancies, a car accident and a miscarriage all within two years, I was pretty low. The instant connection with Andy and the show was a prescription no doctor could write. It lifted me from a dark place, and although I don't want to appear melodramatic or a drama queen, it was a tonic easily digested.

Finding out more about Andy and that he was a devoted family man was refreshing and both my husband and I looked forward to watching Sparty each week and then jumping online to share thoughts with friends.

Andy, you have no idea the difference you made to me, just one little lassie from Scotland who was having a tough time of it. Through your journey I realized that I needed to get up and go grab the world with both hands, to stop wallowing in self-pity and to be grateful for what I had and not the things I had lost, and to start appreciating the finer things in life: I have an amazing, fantastic and gorgeous husband and the most beautiful daughter who surprises me every day.

Thank you, Andy, for coming into my life and for allowing me to share your and your family's journey.

Andy Whitfield 1971-2011

I hope that the love and support shown from all your fans can offer some comfort to your beautiful wife Vashti and your gorgeous kids Jesse Red and Indigo Sky.

Now I have Vashti's blogs to energize my days and again, for this I am truly honoured! Much love!

—*Shelley Aitken*
Alva, Scotland

My Darling,

Months have passed. I don't really know where the time has gone. I think of you and I feel so numb. I'm still so sad about your loss. I think of you every day—I pray for Vashti, Jesse and Indigo, your mum, dad and Laura.

That's all I hear now, people getting cancer. I don't know what's going on, but all I know is that you will always be my champion, my hero. I will always love you, no matter what. It's just a shame we didn't know you for very long, but what we had was awesome. I'm just still very sad.

Rest well in the kingdom of heaven. Promise me this: that you will watch over us and protect us all, because we all still love you so much.

God bless you Andy, and God bless Vashti and the children. Big hugs and love always.

—*Irene*
London

TRIBUTE

Andy,

You were the shining star that has enlightened us with all your splendor, with all your being, with all your strength. You came to us to get to know you, to let us know what a decent human, perfect person you were.

You came to us like thunder that echoed around the world and woke us up to the sense of life and to show us the wonderful man and human being that you were.

Now you've gone to live in the house of God, because He needed your wings and took you, but too early. People— sensitive, nice, beautiful like you—are those who have known defeat, suffering, hurt. You had a sensibility, an understanding of life that you completed with kindness, compassion and a deep love. You were great in everything.

But the thunder that woke us up, it left another mark: loneliness, because without you there is no smile; the world has darkened, it's not blue, because you took it all in your eyes. The color has changed, our days have changed, vision of life has changed.

Now everything is colorless, is living day by day, thinking of you, praying for you. Life is very unfair. You know, Andy, I wanted to meet you here and not on that side. Here, I wanted to see you smile, dream, win and be happy.

Without you, Andy, a lot of people ask why? And I also ask WHY? Why you, Andy?

You know, Andy, we greatly miss you. You are the star that will always light our souls, our hearts. You will always be present in our lives, forever, Andy.

—*Lavinia Goretti Carmona*
Lisbon, Portugal

Andy Whitfield 1971-2011

Can't believe you've been gone for months. I still think of you every day, but now instead of feeling hurt and pain when I see pictures of you I can smile, just a little. I have an image of you sitting on a cloud with those broken butterfly wings now healed into magnificent angels' wings, no longer in pain, watching over Vashti, Jesse and Indigo. Your inner beauty matched your outer beauty, a rare quality. Andy you were such a special person, you have been an inspiration for many including myself. XXX

—Storm
Tewkesbury, England

TRIBUTE

Andy's Incredible Magnetic Presence
Explained by a Professor of Chemistry

The Phenomenon of Andymagnetism

Andymagnetic radiation" is a combination of oscillating magnetic and seductive fields, which propagate through space, carrying energy, smiles and love from one place to another. Unlike other types of waves—like sound—which require a material medium to propagate, Andymagnetic radiation can propagate also through vacuum…from the most recondite places of the Universe.

The theoretical study and understanding of the Andymagnetic radiation is called "Andyfansdynamic," a subfield of the whole amazing phenomenon that is "Andymagnetism."

When "Andymagnetic radiation" impacts on a Fan molecule (FAN), this radiation is absorbed to produce a Fan excited molecule (FAN*) of a higher energy content. This is a quite nice, but an unstable state for the molecule, therefore, the FAN* usually tries to return to its "fundamental state" by means of a re-emission of radiation that provokes a change of the vibrational states (aka "shaking"), which is expressed in an increase of the temperature of FAN (Andymagnetic radiation transformed into heat and Love).

Overexposure to this energetic and wonderful radiation is not harmful at all, so no need to be concerned, because the more exposure, the more excitement and the more number of changes in vibrational states, implies more Heat and much more Love.

—Prof. Inés B.
Seville, Spain

Andy Whitfield 1971-2011

Dearest Andy

Every sunrise you fill up my thoughts
With so much love
With so much pain
Only to know that you
have become one with heaven.

I felt your atoms
From the sigh of your breath.
I don't need your physical form
For nature has taken that away.

I crave your smile.
I crave your thoughts.
I crave you
For there is no more.

But you are always here
In my thoughts.
You speak of love
To wash away the darkest hour.

—*Cathy Dacera*
Alabama, USA

I cannot get these thoughts of you out of my head. I am so sad to think of this world without you in it. Such an amazing actor, husband, father and friend. I am amazed by your ability to truly connect with people that have never met you, but who feel this deep connection with you as if they have known you forever.

Such a remarkable person with your dream of life coming true and to have it all taken away... I just don't understand. My only comfort is knowing you are no longer in pain. You are free, my beautiful butterfly, with wings no longer broken. I will never forget you.

—*Naomi Lynn Ocala*
Florida, USA

Like the contributors to this tribute and thousands of others around the world, I, too, believe Andy Whitfield was an exceptional person. Though we never actually "knew" him, he gave the impression of being able to open a window to his soul, and made us believe that we knew who he really was, both as the character of Spartacus and as himself.

Beyond his obvious talent and physical beauty was the astonishing breadth of his influence on those who connected with him, from the people he worked with to those of us who only came to know him through our TV screens, and no doubt many people who interacted with him in other parts of his life.

To me it seems that Andy's energy had a great deal to do with the amazing way *Spartacus* came together with such a dynamic combination of talent—in all departments—that resulted in the whole being far more than the sum of its parts. I imagine everyone involved the the production rose to and conquered challenges they'd never expected and learned new things in the process.

The wonderfully talented actors, who seem to have deeply appreciated Andy, have come to the public's

Andy Whitfield 1971-2011

attention through their work on *Spartacus* and will find, I'm sure, amazing opportunities in the future which many of us will follow. Stephen DeKnight and Rob Tapert have new projects coming up. I'm sure even the CGI people have developed new effects and ways to work with them. I'm guessing the stunt people, the trainers, costume and set departments have all gained and excelled through their work on this series. Those of us who love Andy can't help but believe that he had some influence, no matter how small, on all of it.

Like ripples on the mirrored surface of a pond, Andy's energy seems to be moving ever outward from the source. Now, though he is no longer with us, his influence continues. With the upcoming *Be Here Now* documentary, there is no doubt he will continue to reach out and touch thousands and thousands new people, many who may never have heard of him or *Spartacus, Blood and Sand*, but who will be moved and inspired by his spirit and his struggle with the disease that took him from us.

I'm so grateful to have "experienced" the connection. I hope I'm still here for his next go around and am able to recognize him for who he is when he arrives!

—*Annette Chaudet*
Wyoming, USA

TRIBUTE

Valentine Thoughts From Fans
February 2012
Valentine Poems

Every Night must break into an Eternal Dawn

Epigraph:

Luego pienso que simplemente no te he perdido,
solo cambiaste tu traje de mundo para fundirte
en la vida
y en el palpitar eterno de la tierra que solo exhala
vitalidad y belleza
luego pienso, que tu sonrisa se ha vuelto música,
que aun cuando tus labios no la llevan
esta ha migrado al sol,
al cantar de los pájaros en la mañana
y a los inconfundibles cantos que se escuchan
solo cuando cae la noche

Translation:

Now I simply think that I have not lost you,
only that you have changed your worldly suit
to melt yourself into life
and into the eternal heartbeat of the earth
that only exhales vitality and beauty.
Now I think that your smile has turned into music,
that even when your lips don't carry it,
it has drifted to the sun,
to the singing of the birds in the morning and
to the unmistakable songs that are heard
only when night falls.

Andy Whitfield 1971-2011

To Vashti Whitfield
and Her Amazing Grace and Strength

The sun has risen
and all I can see is the absence of your light.
As the day goes on
I can feel the wind and how it caresses my skin,
and suddenly I realize
it is your hand slowly passing through my cheek.
As the day when we met and I could just smile.
the twilight comes, and with it,
the crimson glow that paints the blue sky,
turning it into a dark blue
that reminds me of your scent.
A scent that could make me shiver,
A scent that could keep me drowning,
every day...every night.
Then I feel the warm embrace of the moon,
shining in the middle of the sky
as you did whenever you smiled,
like a lighthouse in the middle of my endless ocean
of fears that you would push away.
The warm embrace of the moon
that reminds me of your arms around me,
of your soft kisses and your sweet voice
telling me it will all be alright.
Every night must break, and I had to be awakened
from the beautiful dream of your love.
I must stop the ride and look back for a minute,
knowing that we will meet again

Once again your light will shower me with strength.
Once again your scent will make me drown.
Once again your smile
will make me smile and your tears will make me cry.

TRIBUTE

I'll be yours once again
and know that you'll forever be mine,
my angel, my guardian and my lover,
my friend and my mentor,
my Deep Ocean and Eternal Sky.
You will always be the rock
that will keep me strong and going till we meet again.
But for now, I'll just let the wind caress my skin,
the moon enlighten me.
I'll just let the twilight and the crimson glow
paint my darkest nights
'cause I know you are there,
because I know you are the beauty,
a beauty so ravishing that it can eclipse
the atrocity of the world that now I live in.
For now, I'll be your voice, my eyes will see
what you'd see and I'll say what you'd say
till your voice speaks for itself
and your eyes see their reflection in mine,
Cause every night must break into an eternal dawn,
an eternal dawn that we'll share.

—Luisa Ramos W.
Medellin, Colombia

A Poem For Andy...

Lament For A Warrior.

The Warrior sleeps, the battle fought not won.
From high up he watches, his job not done.
Guarding his loved ones has just begun.

—Susan Rebecca Peel
United Kingdom

Andy Whitfield 1971-2011

A Poem for a Special Person

A special person you only meet once in a lifetime
maybe you won't meet at all...
as it happened to me with you...over all.
One day I saw you on screen and immediately
I was in love with a rare human being.
I was not able any more to divert my eyes
from your eyes and I'm not saying lies.
Suddenly I knew you were somewhere
and I have found out what was there in you,
all that I'd like to find in me and in a man too;
everything was in your person:
talent, sensitivity, education, love,
grace and a very beautiful face.
I was happy to know
you were in the world with me...so
my life seemed better to me, not worse
and I'm honored to write you these words.
You were able to cancel my pains,
you've taken them away with the rains.
Photos and videos are all I have about you,
while I look at the screen or a picture too
I think you now are distant...it is true!
I don't want close my eyes ever for an instant,
I want that my attention on you is constant.
When I think of you, my mind goes blank
from my thought that now I understand,
when I see you...my friend,
as you move and express yourself and then
while you sweat, breathe,
while you talk...my sweet man.
My heart misses a beat every time I hear your voice...
and I forget what is the noise.
You have come on a beautiful day into my life,

TRIBUTE

in silence, but on a horrible day
you're gone and I'm here with your absence.
A deafening noise now never leaves me
and I want to tell you graciously:
It's my soul that cries its pain
and your name forever:
ANDY.

—Marina
Italy

Did you know how much we cared for you
Did you know our words were true
Did you know we all adored you
Did you know we loved you too
Did you know what a special man you were
Did you feel that from our love
Did you know to us the world stood still
When you were taken high above
Please know that we adore you still
Please know this to be true
Please know we keep you in our heart
For always...Only you...

—Sandra James
Eastcalder, Westlothian, Scotland

Andy Whitfield 1971-2011

From a distance the first time
I heard your warm voice
I started to shiver
I had no choice.
My feet carried me
toward my TV-screen
Your face! The most beautiful
I've ever seen.
With each minute passing,
you're pulling me in
to see and feel
your life deep within.
And when you're in the arena fighting
I find myself yelling,
"Move away fast as lightning!"
Each episode I always fear
that Claudius Glaber's coming near.
As I watch and memorize
every line, every scene
You're ever becoming
the man of my dream!
From this day forward,
I make a promise to thee
You will never ever have
a bigger fan than me!

—*Abir Mansur*
Sweden

TRIBUTE

Per TE...

Il suono della TUA voce è la mia preghiera
di tutti i giorni.
Amo semplicemente il pensiero di TE.
Mi manca tutto senza più il TUO sguardo...
e non esiste un altro posto a cui appartengo.
Il vento soffia sibilando il TUO nome...
e il dolce TUO ricordo
appartiene all'eternità.
Amo pensare il TUO respiro scorrere
tra le mie mani sul TUO viso...
Tutto ora scorre in silenzio...
e c'è un silenzio dove ritrovarti...nel mio cuore...

Translation:

For You

The sound of your voice is my prayer every day.
I love just the thought of you.
I miss everything without your gaze...
and there is no other place to which I belong.
The wind is whispering your name...
and your sweet memory
belongs to eternity.
I like to think of your breath
flowing through my hands on your face...
Everything now runs in silence...
and it's silent where I find you...in my heart...

—Maddalena
Italy

Andy Whitfield 1971-2011

You will shine in our hearts
as a star that shines in the sky.
Andy you're the shining star.
And you will shine forever in our hearts, in eternity.
Andy we love you so much.
Andy we miss you so much.
Andy Whitfield Forever, Always and in Eternity!

—*Diana Ioana Gheorghe*
Giulianova, Italy

Andy Whitfield

A slave to your inspirations
Need you here still!
Dreaming of an everlasting kiss
Your sweet priceless lips untouched.
When love prevails, fear departs
How many phrases will you speak for there are no more
I have been seeking a love like this for I must truly live
Tenderness of your skin I see it glow
Fragrance I smell seducing my soul
In you I see the essence that invades and touches me.
Endless thoughts of your silent solitude, I weep.
Love vanished into an ocean of honey for I must drink.
Dearer to me you are than my own sweet soul.

—*Cathy Dacera*
Alabama, USA

TRIBUTE

Believe in Angels, Believe in You

Believe in angels.
How difficult a task when you have lost faith...
Give faith back to me with your nice eyes,
                    your loving smile, your presence.
The angels protect, angels guide, angels embrace...
I was looking for an angel, a white angel
                            in this mad world.
A pure angel, full of love, a guardian angel...
I was looking for you all my life.
You are my guardian angel.

My faith vanished for moments...
moments of uncertainty, lost moments when you left.

When I didn't look, I found you...
When I found you, you left...
When you left I lost again...I lost my faith...

A moment, a memory, a feeling...
No matter how long you've been in this world...
No matter how many angels may come
No matter your absence be eternal
You came to me, leaving a touching mark
an indelible mark for eternity

To ask an angel to live on this earth for longer
is to demand the impossible.
An angel must fly, an angel must depart from earth.
No place for angels in this world.
Angels live in Heaven where you are now.

You, my angel, you have gone and you're free now.

Andy Whitfield 1971-2011

I'm chained to you and someday I will see...
No matter when, how or where...
My blessing is to know that you existed
and at the end of my days
I will meet you again.

I believe in angels now.
Dedicated to you, my angel...
dedicated to my white angel...
Dedicated to you, Andy Whitfield...

—Elizabeth Segarra
Spain

The True Strength of a Beautiful Fighter

To be strong is to know how to suffer in silence.
To be strong is to radiate happiness
when you feel like crying.
To be strong is trying to forgive someone
who does not deserve forgiveness.
Being strong is expected
when you do not believe in the return.
Being strong is to keep calm
in the moment of desperation.
Being strong is to show joy
when you do not feel.
Being strong is to make someone happy
when we have our heart in pieces.
To be strong is to be silent and to smile when the ideal
would be to scream for all one's anguish.
To be strong is to comfort when you need comfort.

TRIBUTE

Being strong is laughing with eyes full of tears.
Being strong is to have faith when it is hard to believe.
Being strong is to transmit courage
even when you feel fear.
That is why, even with the hard and difficult reality
You, Andy, you have been strong as a true warrior.

You were an example of courage and strength and you
will never be forgotten, beautiful Blue Eyes.

To you and for you, always, Andy Whitfield.

—Lavinia Goretti Carmona
Lisbon, Portugal

For Vashti.

Listen carefully and you'll hear his whisper on the wind.
Stand completely still and you can feel his breath
on your skin,
Look to the sky on a clear summer day,
you'll see the deep blue of his eyes,
and you'll feel his strength in the waves of the sea.

His smile is contagious and his joy is heard
in the laughter of a child.
His anger is shown in the force of a hurricane,
tornado or exploding volcano,
His sadness is heard in the cries of a nation.
You'll feel his tears with every raindrop
falling on your face.

Andy Whitfield 1971-2011

His spirit and courage are within his children,
but his love and determination are within you.
Andy will forever be a legend.

—*Sara Talajlo*
Colchester, UK

I will make a casket of my soul for your soul,
a home of my heart for your beauty.
My chest will be a grave for your pains.
I will love you like the prairies love the Spring,
I will live in you the life of a butterfly
under the rays of the sun.
I will sing your name as the valley sings
the echo of the fields.
I will listen to the language of your soul
like the beach listens to the story of the waves.
I'll quench my thirst by contemplating your pictures
every day of my life.

—*Marina*
Italy

TRIBUTE

Epilogue

Many people, myself included, expressed thanks to Andy and Vashti Whitfield for letting us experience Andy's brilliant and inspiring presence.

We saw a Man become a Fighter, a Champion, a Hero and ultimately a Legend.

Little did we know that Andy and Vashti's greatest gift was yet to be unveiled.

The documentary *Be Here Now* will share Andy's most challenging and final fight as we are allowed to partake in the intimate journey of his last months on this Earth.

The true legacy he graced us with is the profound wisdom: to live life to the fullest, NOW.

We bow our head in humble gratitude
Namaste

—*Irena Kyd*
New York

Lightning Source UK Ltd.
Milton Keynes UK
UKOW041820031012

200032UK00012B/155/P